VOLUME III

WOODSTOCK
ORIGINALS

VOLUME III

WOODSTOCK
ORIGINALS

Stories and Poems
from
The Byrdcliffe Writers

Edited by
Dr. Joseph Keefe

Editor in Chief
Joseph Keefe

Managing Editor
Gene Patterson

Associate Editors
Adele LeBlanc, Tara McCarthy,
Scott Morgan, R. L. Tucker

Library of Congress Card Number 84-151442
ISBN 0-9625244-0-9

Designed by Broadview Media, Woodstock, New York
Cover design by Don Wright

Printed in the United States of America

The Byrdcliffe Writers
112 Byrdcliffe Road, Woodstock, NY 12498

1990

Contents

Introduction

Welcome to the third volume of *Woodstock Originals*! We hope that the readers who were so pleased with volume one and two will be equally pleased with this effort. We have not changed our approach. Once again we are attempting to entertain you with stories and poems that we believe are of high literary quality and yet are somewhat different from those found in currently popular books and magazines. Our ideal is still the spirit of the Byrdcliffe art colony founded by Ralph Whitehead.

In 1984, we published our first volume of *Woodstock Originals*, a collection of twenty stories and eight poems. A small book, only 115 pages, it celebrated the vitality and imagination of a dozen writers, all members of a writing class that first began meeting in the Byrdcliffe barn in the summer of 1977. That book marked the beginning of a new phase in the development of the writing group.

Before the publication of *Woodstock Originals*, the writers wrote bits and pieces of experience and brought them in for discussion. Although the discussions were lively, some of the writers soon began to feel that something essential was missing. As Flora Patterson said, "We are like a choir practicing and practicing for a concert that is never given." *Woodstock Originals*, then, became the group's first concert.

Our second volume, *Woodstock Originals* II, was published in 1987. Woodstock Historian Alf Evers wrote a brief foreword and Gail Godwin favored us with complimentary comments such as the following: "Like the town of Woodstock itself, this second volume of *Woodstock Originals* teems with the variety and energy that results from people of many different backgrounds and experiences coming together for an artistic venture."

Like the second volume, the third volume of *Woodstock*

Originals also teems with that variety and energy.

On a more personal note, let me say that I did not realize when Flora Patterson asked me to teach an informal writing class in 1977 that the class would ever lead to anything like *Woodstock Originals* I, much less *Woodstock Originals* II and III. Much of the credit must go to Flora. She organized the original class and realized, before any of the rest of us, the need for a publication to demonstrate the talents of the various writers. Also a great deal of credit must go to the husbands, and wives, and significant others who gave the writers time to bring these collections into being. I, personally, know how often my wife, Jane, has had to put her own wishes and plans aside so I could work with the writers.

Since 1977, my association with the Byrdcliffe Writers has been an extremely satisfying one. Working with them has enriched my life and will, I hope, continue to enrich my life long after the time has come for me to relinquish my baton so the choir may respond to a new choirmaster.

In closing, let me quote a short passage from my own introduction to *Woodstock Originals* I. It tells how I feel about works of art such as those produced at the original Byrdcliffe art colony and in the small studios around Woodstock even today. And, of course, among those works of art I would include the three volumes produced by the Byrdcliffe Writers.

> ...The handwoven shawl, irregular in size, with threads both delicate and vivid in hue. The glazed pitcher of individual design, shimmering with an elusive blue. These are precious things and are not to be despised because the artists are people like you and me. We might just as well despise a home-cooked holiday dinner, the table brimming with delights perfected by years of cooking with love, because the cook has no great worldly reputation. Without such precious things, handwoven cloth and blue pitchers and home-cooked meals, life would lose much of its savor. As Ralph Whitehead knew, and John Ruskin before him, we must participate in art if we are to truly enjoy it.
>
> —Joseph Keefe

Afraid of the Dark
Scott Morgan

My son is asleep, finally. I walk into his room, and turn off the lamp by his bed, leaving the small Mickey Mouse nightlight plugged in at the base of the wall, with Mickey's smiling face glowing eerily.

Robbie is five, and recently he's become afraid of the dark. Before he goes to bed, he takes me by the hand, and together we check all the closets in the house, searching among the clothes, shoes, toys, folding chairs and old curtain rods for anyone hiding. When he's sure no one's inside, he'll shut the closet hard, then stare at it, his small brows tightening, eyes doubtful, as though he knows the things he truly fears can't be stopped by doors.

Each day, he seems to find more and more things about the dark that scare him: the vampire in the attic, the bogey under the bed, the ghost in the hall. Last evening he asked me to close his bedroom curtains.

"Why? What are you afraid of?"

"Monsters."

"That's silly," I told him. "There are no monsters."

"Look!"

He pointed to the window, and there were the monsters, staring back at us, half-blackened reflections of ourselves in a shadowy room, inhabiting a negative world.

Sometimes, like tonight, I wake up, and can't fall back asleep. It feels like someone's pulling me by the hair, so that my eyes bug out. I walk around the house, in and out of Robbie's room, to the kitchen, den, living room. I stare out the picture window at the backyard, the white birches a tangle of branches and trunks, the sky in constant motion, clouds racing dizzyingly across the bright November moon.

Wherever I go these days, when I look at people I see private worlds in motion, like molecules—wheels of spinning sadness, held in some order, but separate, separate worlds of grief. And the universe seems to need these griefs, or why was life ordered this way?

I have a small vitamin C bottle, half filled with Valium, locked in a metal filing box on the top shelf of the den closet. My mother in Brooklyn keeps big pill jars of Valium on the spice rack in her kitchen, and when I visit, she gives me fifteen or twenty, for nerves, in case I need them. "They're good to have around," she tells me, tapping them out like little yellow candies, the way Robbie carefully taps out his watermelon Nerds for a friend. I don't take them often, but it comforts me to think of that bottle, tucked away like a talisman between my tax and mortgage papers. And sometimes, when I'm racing from Lenox to Pittsfield to meet a client, my mind filled with figures slowly embroidering themselves around my thoughts until they're a tight black web, I like to anticipate the sweet dulled peace in the evening from taking one, or two.

My wife doesn't know about the Valium, but we've been keeping our minds to ourselves lately.

Karen was pregnant last spring. She'd sit for hours on the living room couch, chewing the ends of her blond hair, her eyes distant, as though she were staring into another dimension, trying to fathom its secrets. Robbie seemed more excited than threatened by the idea of a brother or sister, and sorted through his old toys for which ones to give the baby: fancy rattles, a Mother Goose mobile, a bounce-back clown with bells inside. But he also began playing with them again with a particular seriousness, for hours sometimes, as if trying hard to recapture some pleasure he knew he'd lost.

When the baby was four months, I went with Karen to her doctor, so I could hear the heartbeat for the first time. The doctor squeezed a jelly over Karen's stomach, and placed his stethoscope against her, but all he could hear was the noise of the placenta. He tried for five minutes to find the heartbeat. Karen smiled, and said, "I know the baby's alive, because I felt it last night."

"What did you feel?" he asked, squeezing more jelly onto

her, and sliding the metal cap of the stethoscope around to find a better place to listen.

"I don't know. A kind of flubbery feeling. Like a 'blip, blip.' I felt the same thing with Robbie."

She seemed so sure, that I wasn't too worried. The doctor said, "The placenta might be masking the sounds of the heartbeat, but I'd like you to go to the hospital for a sonogram, to be sure."

As we were leaving, I asked him if they'd tell us what they found out at the hospital.

"If everything's okay, they'll tell you right there. If the doctor says you have to speak to me, then you'll know something's wrong."

We don't live at the center of life, we live at the margin, at the farthest edge. The vast field of living is all on one side, and seems to go on forever, but no matter how hard we try to move into that infinite, sane, stable territory, we can't escape the edge.

When Robbie bathes, he likes to float on his back, arms at his sides, his face all but submerged, dark hair swaying out like sea grass. As I watch him, I feel how close death is. Three minutes, five minutes, and all that giggling, grinning promise of life could end. We live at the margin of life, and we're not allowed any mistakes.

"Don't lay in the water like that," I tell him.

"Daddy, I like to. You're not being fair. Why can't I?"

What am I going to say, that it makes me imagine him dead, drowned?

"It doesn't matter why. Please stop it. Now."

He sits up, scowling. Maybe it would be better to tell him the truth, but I'd rather have him deal with a willful, possibly irrational authority, whose laws he'll spend a lifetime trying to understand, than infect him with my fears.

I hear Robbie groan in his sleep. I'm still thinking about the metal filing box and the bottle of Valium, giving myself all the reasons why I deserve to take some now, but I hurry into his room.

The blanket is off, and he's shivering. I pull it over him, but he kicks it away immediately. He was a cesarean baby, and

Karen wonders if that has something to do with his kicking off the blanket every night, as though he might, in sleep, still be trying to break his way out of the tight world he was in, with its hole too small to slide out of.

Karen and I didn't talk much on the drive to the hospital. The day was clear and warm, the sky brilliant, the landscape flush with summer growth.

The lab technician, a smiling young woman, brought us into the sonogram room.

"Here," she said, handing Karen a white dressing gown, "you put this on, and I'll be right back."

Karen lay down on the examining table, rubbing her belly, as though it were a bottle with a genie inside, and she was making a wish.

The technician came in, turned on the machine, and shut the lights. She squirted the same kind of jelly the doctor had onto Karen's stomach, so that I began to imagine the jelly was the conductor of life itself. I kept thinking, If she only uses enough of that stuff, everything will be all right. She placed the transducer onto Karen, and it was like watching a transmission from the moon. The picture shifted wildly for a moment, and then we saw the light, blurred fetus curled inside.

"Look," I said, "there's the heartbeat."

"Where?" she asked, in a neutral voice.

"There. Where it's pumping."

"That's your wife's aorta."

Karen held my hand, but I couldn't look at her. I kept staring at the screen, at the tiny shape like a white-suited astronaut, afloat in its own universe. The technician left the room, and brought the lab doctor in. He was a short, brisk man from India. He nodded to us, examined the screen, asked the technician some questions, took notes, and then went out.

The technician helped Karen clean up, then turned on the lights as she left the room. The white fluorescence, jumping out of darkness, hurt my eyes, and made the world dreamlike. I pinched myself, harder and harder, until the nail marks formed ovals on my arm. "Come on, wake up. You can wake yourself from this if you try!"

The doctor came back in. For some reason, I shook his hand, as if somehow that would sway him to give a better report. He seemed surprised

"How's the baby?"

"I will call your doctor for you," he said, in his clipped, precise English, "and he will explain the results."

This is how I used to see my life: I had constructed a kind of tower for myself in an emotional sea, and I watched events from above, observing, commenting, criticizing. I believed I had the power to control what happened, the way a player makes moves on a gameboard. My family, when I was growing up in Brooklyn, had a certain solidity, the pillars all in place— two sets of grandparents, parents, and on top, me. I thought I was exempt from the kinds of tragedies and sorrows I saw around me: a friend's father dying of a heart attack, parents divorcing, a girl in my class who had been born with no left hand. But I've learned no one is exempt. I've written that on a piece of paper, which I keep in my wallet: NO ONE IS EXEMPT. Karen tells me I was just blind to what went on in my own family, willfully avoiding reality. "Why did you think your mother took Valium all those years?"

When I was a little younger than Robbie, I owned a three foot tall toy stuffed wolf in peppermint-striped overalls, with a menacing smile and cherry red tongue. I called him Willie the Wolf. One day, I had my father tie a cord around his neck, and hang him over my bedroom door. I think I got the idea from watching an episode of Wagon Train on TV.

That night I woke up, and in the shallow light from my Davy Crockett lamp I saw Willie, grinning down at me from the top of the door, his red tongue hanging out, head slightly bent, arms loose at his sides. I screamed.

I heard my father say, "Don't go in now. You'll just baby him."

"What do you want from him?" my mother demanded. "He's only four."

"I didn't get away acting like that when I was four."

She came into my room.

"What's wrong with my baby?"

"I'm scared of him!" I cried, pointing to Willie.

My mother took him down, and untied the rope around his neck. She looked towards the other room, her dark hair mussed, her pretty face scowling.

"I don't know why he does things like this," she said. "He should know better," and I had the feeling she thought stringing up Willie was my father's idea. But I said nothing.

She climbed into bed with me, and smoothed my hair. Her skin was still warm with sleep, and I curled against her.

"You don't have to be scared now. Mommy's here, and she won't let anything happen to you."

I still played with Willie after that night, but I never trusted him again, which, when I think of it, doesn't make sense, since I was the one who betrayed him.

We left Robbie with a friend, and went back to the hospital the next morning. Karen was given Prostaglandin to induce labor, and we spent fourteen hours in the maternity ward while Karen, drugged with Demerol, dozing, crying, soiling her sheets, tried to push the dead baby from her body. When it finally came, I heard a squirting, plopping sound, and then the nurse wrapped it in a sheet.

The doctor asked me, "Would you like to see it?"

I shook my head no.

"It sometimes helps if you look."

I watched as the sheet was opened, and saw the fetus: small, half formed, bloody, stringy, yet still human, with dark spaces in the large head where eyes would have formed, and opened.

I held back my tears. It wasn't until later—months later—that I wondered why I hadn't allowed myself to cry. It might have helped. It might have broken the wall inside me that has separated me from Karen since then.

When we told Robbie that night something had happened, and he wouldn't be having a brother or sister after all, he didn't say anything. He sat on the couch, watching his cartoons, but before he went to bed, he gathered all the toys he had put aside, and one by one, slammed them back into his toybox in the closet.

Karen and I were brutal to each other all summer. It was as if, when the dead fetus came out, something came out in us, too, dark and ugly, poisonous.

One night, when I told her she shouldn't get so upset about something (I can't remember what it was. I was often telling her she shouldn't get so upset), she started yelling at me.

"You want me to keep every feeling I have wrapped up, so it doesn't bother you. You'd like it all neat and tidy. Well, I'm not like that, and I'm sick of you trying to make me."

Her whole face looked distorted. I was glad, because the uglier she looked to me, the easier it was to hurt her. "Why shouldn't I want it neat? What's wrong with that? Maybe you make life messier than it has to be. Am I some kind of freak, because I don't want to cheer every time you express your emotions?"

"You're such a cold, self-satisfied son of a bitch! I had to give birth to a dead baby. My baby was dead in me for two weeks, and I didn't even know it! How much emotion am I allowed for that? Have you got that figured out in your ledger?"

She was shivering with anger. I told her, "It was my baby, too. Don't forget that. You're not the only one who feels things!"

"Oh, now you feel things? Since when? To you, the whole thing was just a big joke!"

She stormed into the living room. I followed her. There was a standing lamp between us, and I smashed it to the ground. The bulb popped, consuming us in darkness. We stood there, panting, like two animals ready to spring at each other again.

Robbie was crying in his bed. We seemed to feel his crying, at the same moment, almost more than we heard it. We ran in, and found him huddled under the covers, heaving spasmodically, holding his hands over his ears. We hugged and kissed him.

"Mommies and daddies get mad sometimes with each other," I told him, "just like you do with your friends. But it doesn't mean they don't love each other."

I could see from Robbie's face that he wanted us to prove it, to smile, and kiss, and make him believe what he heard didn't matter. But we couldn't, and I felt ashamed, and I think Karen did too, but our anger was more important.

When I feel a wave of emotion, a suffocating heaving up of pure feeling, I grab onto that moment in the sonogram room, when I knew for sure the baby was dead. The harsh lights, Karen in a chair, hugging her stomach, the lab doctor's cool palm and clipped English as he spoke the exact words, as though from a script, that our doctor said we would hear if something was wrong. I pin it spinning in my consciousness, and it can't get free, and it wears away a groove. I tell myself, "You're afraid to let that moment go, because you know that emotion, hard as it is, but you don't know what's next, you don't know where to go from here."

I think of all the bad moments from the time I was a kid, wearing away grooves inside my head—fights, arguments, humiliations—and they're all spinning away, and maybe I'm afraid of them, too, afraid of what would happen if I really let them go.

Robbie calls out, "Mommy! Daddy! I'm all alone!"

I run in, and a minute later, Karen comes too.

"What's wrong?" she asks him, smoothing his hair, just as my mother used to do with me.

"I'm afraid. I don't want to be by myself."

"Come on," she says, "we'll go in the big bed."

She carries him into our room, and they lie down together. I watch them for a few moments, and I'm about to walk out again when Robbie pats the space next to him, and says, "You stay too." Karen looks up at me. The room is dim, except for the moonlight, drifting in between the curtains, and I can't make out her expression.

I climb into the bed. Robbie spreads his body so that it touches each of us. His eyes are wide open.

"Back to sleep," I tell him, but his eyes stay open, staring at the ceiling, and I feel as if we're all being carried on a rising swell of grief. "It's all right," I say, more softly, brushing my fingers against his cheek. "We're all here together. You don't have to be afraid."

The Dog Psychologist
Susan Sutliff Brown

Dulling gold and orange leaves were restless in the chill
October air the day my mother tried to hire a dog psychologist.
I remember how the day broke with a cold edge. I started
thinking about ice glazing the windows in February. The wood
stove would work well enough when father scraped out the
ashes and set the fire each night and morning. But the house
would be gray and chilly when mother and I arrived home in
the afternoons. "Oh dear, the fire's out, isn't it?" she would say.
Then she'd climb under her down quilt and bury herself in
books on saving the wetlands or "making friends with your
emotions." But that was okay. Once I was old enough to carry
in the logs and light matches, I set the fire in the afternoons.

The new dog was sort of like the wood stove—another thing
that was supposed to make our shelter safe and secure but that
needed people to make it work. And the first person the dog
needed—my mother had decided—was a psychologist.

"Just how expensive?" my father had asked that Saturday
morning as he laced up his work boots.

My mother stopped twisting the fringe on her shawl and
began to fill a teapot from the tap. "I don't know. 'Expensive'
is all I know. We'll just talk to him. We're desperate. And
everyone I've talked to says he works miracles."

"The miracle, Linda, is how we will pay for such a non-
essential item." Ever since my mother had begun using her
middle name "Violet," her eyes narrowed when my father
called her "Linda." My middle name was Janice (after Grandma
Janice) so there was little danger of my switching names in late
life. I was content with "Greta."

My mother began rattling around the kitchen picking up
stray cups and pots. "I hope you're not planning on moving any
more of the paintings out to the studio with you. Remember—

we agreed not to change the house. For Greta's sake. And don't worry about the cost. Watchdogs need training, and, as long as I'm living here alone, I need a watchdog. You know I can't sleep when I'm alone in a house. You know that. The slightest noise and I'm dialing 911."

My father carried his coffee cup to the sink. "Well, why not? I remember how well the hypnotherapy worked on you, and the acu-yoga, and microcosmic meditation. Can't argue with success." Mother opened and closed a cupboard door without taking anything out.

Actually, my father was wrong. It was called "microcosmic *orbit* meditation." And he didn't know that mother had also taken psychodrama training and a workshop in stress management/assertiveness. One time she dragged me along to the Shiatsu Health Emporium where the Japanese massage therapist was trained in "deep tissue release foot reflexology."

I tried not to notice that my father's calling Mother "Linda" and mentioning the acu-yoga was swirling through the kitchen like the bite of an unexpected cool breeze. Since my father had moved to the studio three months earlier, at the beginning of what my mother called a "trial separation," they had managed to be polite—almost formal—to one another, especially in front of me. We still had meals together, and my parents shared the same paper over coffee in the morning so "we could still keep the family together." One Saturday my father made blueberry banana pancakes and Mother and I ate them and said they were good—even though we knew he'd rescued the speckled bananas just before my mother threw them away.

The screen door slapped shut as my mother followed my father out the door. "Well, I've called him anyway. We'll just talk to him. Certainly there's a way to interact non-violently with a domestic animal. We're civilized people." Her voice grew more robust as my father angled out of earshot.

The three of us stood on the back porch—my mother, me, and our new dog—a squirming, twelve-week-old Labrador retriever mix named Beowulf with paws as big as sundials. Mother's long, sandy hair whipped about her face in the autumn wind and she pulled her shawl tight about her gauze blouse and peasant skirt. I was afraid to look at her. We both stared straight ahead at specks of macadam through the huge tangle of tree limbs until the dog psychologist rumbled his clean, red, pickup truck up our driveway and parked parallel to the rhododendron hedge. At the exact moment that the engine stopped, the German shepherd that had been balanced in the open truck bed, pulled itself onto the roof of the cab with a movement as smooth as water running uphill. Then the dog stretched out, a figurehead on a pickup truck.

Leonard Roth, a man who managed to be well-groomed but dark, hairy, and burly at the same time, swung gracefully down from the running board, and stared with the intensity of a drug abuse counselor into my mother's eyes as he announced his name and then pronounced hers, "Mrs. Hill." Granted I was only eleven, but I might as well have been in my room with the door shut.

"Please call me 'Violet.' This is the dog. We're desperate. She has housebroken herself. That's not the problem. What we need is a dog that will let itself in and out, stay close to home, bark if strangers appear, but for God's sake never bite—that is essential—and stop jumping up and stop chewing everything."

Leonard Roth walked smoothly past Mother and me, directly to Beowulf, crouched, picked up the puppy, and began to swing Beowulf slowly back and forth by a huge flap of neck skin. The dog drooped, limp as a rag doll. The dog psychologist then stretched Beowulf out on the lawn and began to probe her feet, teeth, and stomach with what were clearly educated fingers. The dog just lay motionless, an ecstatic convert, staring up at Leonard Roth.

"How did you do that?" my mother squeaked, but the dog psychologist just shifted positions and examined the speckled undersides of Beowulf's ears, one by one. Then he murmured "Hm." My mother backed up with a hiccup. My father was always able to silence her by raising his hand like an Indian greeting. It was right after the assertiveness training, just before Father moved out, that I caught my mother in front of a mirror practicing confronting him. She was telling him that he had to learn to "listen," that what she had to say was important, that she was a "human being." As I lay in bed that night listening to the crickets, I prayed that she hadn't seen my face flash for a moment beside hers in the glass. She would have been embarrassed.

After swinging the limp dog back into the air and tucking Beowulf into the bend of one arm, the dog psychologist turned to the truck. In a voice that sounded like the first soft rumble of distant thunder, he said, "Greta, come here."

I jumped, but caught myself when I realized that his dog had my name. For some reason Mother failed to notice this astonishing fact, but instead stared without blinking as the shepherd trotted to Leonard Roth's side and stood calmly waiting for more commands. At the order, "Greta, lie down," the shepherd gracefully bent backwards, dropping to a perfect "lying" position without even flexing a shoulder or adjusting a paw.

I suddenly noticed that my father, who had been chopping wood on a hill about 100 yards away, was resting on his ax, watching.

After first rubbing his hand over Beowulf's round under-belly, Leonard Roth set the puppy on the grass next to the docile Greta. When Beowulf circled the strange dog twice and then began growling like a sputtering motor and leaping in jerks at the unperturbed trespasser, the hairy dog psychologist again murmured "Hm."

In response to the next command, "Greta, stand," the shepherd rose in one liquid movement that looked like a movie of falling dominos played in reverse. At first Beowulf yipped in surprise, and sprawled backwards into a sitting position. Then suddenly the puppy charged forward with a falsetto bark. "Hm," said Leonard Roth.

My mother began to nod. "I knew it. She's atypically aggressive, isn't she? I mean we can't even stop her from nipping little children's feet. And we have lots of friends with children."

For the first time, Leonard Roth looked at my mother. "The heel nipping is pure instinct," he said as he turned back to Beowulf. "Actually, your dog is scoring the heels of her prey or enemies, a purely automatic response to strangers on your property."

"Oh my goodness," my mother said, her hand flying to her mouth. "That's horrible. Absolutely horrible. How do we train her not to that?"

"Unless she is resocialized, this behavior will become more, not less, pronounced. The dog is protecting its family. Dogs are social animals, Mrs. Hill. But your dog is reacting with ancient instincts. Unless the dog is psychologically restructured to live in a human pack—and this household is its pack—it can only operate by what natural responses it is born with." Leonard Roth was the first person I had ever met besides my father who spoke in complete sentences.

I was feeling uncomfortable, too, at the way my mother was punctuating all of these complete sentences with nods of her head. Then she said, "You mean that her natural instinct is to dominate our household until she is trained to understand her role in a human environment?" I cocked my eyebrows at Mother, but she didn't notice.

"I do not 'train' animals, Mrs. Hill. I would resocialize your dog to embrace the security of a subservient role in a human pack," Leonard Roth corrected.

"'Violet,'" my mother corrected.

"I don't know what you know about my work, but if you want your animal trained and dragged on a choke collar, I can't help you." In a voice I could barely hear, Leonard Roth then ordered his dog to "go to the truck, Greta, and mount the roof." There were years of talking-suicides-off-ledges-for-pay in that voice.

The dog psychologist next scanned the yard slowly before looking at our back door. "Now I need to observe the dog's behavior in your home."

"Of course," began my mother, and another waterfall of her questions tumbled off the thick, bushy hair of the back of the dog psychologist's head as he walked into the house ahead of us. He was busy studying the layout of the rooms.

Leonard declined my mother's homegrown herb tea; he accepted a mug of coffee, black. And we all settled primly in the living room, Mother balanced on the edge of the couch curling the long strands of her hair around her finger with her bony feet tucked flat against the couch's wooden skirt. She had been losing weight for over a year now. My father blamed it on aerobics and folk dancing. I slid into the corner, my shoulder blades tensed in case Leonard Roth said "Greta" again, and the puppy, Beowulf, snarled as it tugged at the braided rug. We waited for the dog psychologist to say something.

"Who is that?" Leonard Roth demanded.

"Where? Who?" My mother set down her tea.

"That dog," said Leonard Roth nodding toward our seven-year-old half-deaf spaniel plus, Melville (my father named the dogs), who was sprawled under the love seat.

"Oh," sighed Mother, "that's just Melville. He's no problem."

"Mrs. Hill, if what you want is a dog that is 'no problem,' I can't help you."

"Well, I mean, Melville stays close to home and doesn't attack children. Of course, we do feed and bathe and pet him, but we don't consider that trouble." I moved closer to the couch. Mother was starting to tug at her shawl fringe again.

"You have no relationship with that animal, Mrs. Hill. This dog has no notion of what his role is in this household or of what is expected of him," said the dog psychologist. We all looked at Melville who lifted one eyelid and then sighed and collapsed back into his dreams.

"But we love Melville." I could see Mother gathering her thoughts as she paused for a sip of tea. "Granted the relationship we have with him might be understated, but what kind of relationship do we want with a dog? Goodness. A fourth for bridge?" I smiled, but very carefully, so Leonard Roth wouldn't notice. My mother laughed gaily, waving her slender hand, but Leonard Roth just sat back and took a deep sip of his coffee.

"In human terms, Mrs. Hill, the condition is known as dissonance—equally competing emotions—in this case insecurity and frustration—creating a level of emotional impotence—or, in other words, withdrawal. The dog is so desensitized it does not even engage in a classic inter-male aggression response with the new animal." We all looked at Melville again; he was motionless. My mother quickly scowled at me. Somehow this was my fault.

"But your new dog is the more serious problem," said Leonard Roth. "This young animal has been under tremendous pressure to define her role in this household. She believes that she must protect this house and property even though she is only an infant."

I was feeling especially low about Melville at this point and vowed to pet him more often.

"What I would do," said Leonard Roth, "is help your animal achieve a level of modified learned helplessness so the dog will feel secure and protected by your family. Once she understands the hierarchy in her new pack and I have taught your family the correct stimuli and signals, she will adjust properly into your home." Leonard Roth lifted Beowulf by the scruff of the neck. The puppy swooned, holding her breath for the dog guru's next signal.

"I couldn't agree with you more, Mr. Roth," my mother said, edging forward. "It's just like people. Imagine that," she mused. "All those animals longing for the security of the pack—and wanting to know their role in the family."

"Of course, Mrs. Hill, I cannot do any of this without the commitment of your entire family."

My mother set down her tea again. "That's why my daughter is here, in fact. The puppy is really her dog. She agreed to train it. She wants to. So maybe you should be talking to her. And I really wish you would call me 'Violet.'"

I noticed that Violet didn't tell him my name. And she didn't tell him that we'd added the dog to our pack because she suddenly needed a watchdog. Melville had only barked twice in seven years, once at a paper bag and once at a horse who then stepped on his foot and broke it. Mother had begun campaigning for a second dog when my parents agreed on the "trial separation." Well, not really agreed. The day after Father moved his duffle bag and a few cardboard boxes of books and his razor to the studio, my mother called in sick to work and spent the whole afternoon and night in bed with books she borrowed from her divorced friend Eleanor. So at first, the dog had been my father's fault. Now she was blaming Beowulf on me.

But I accepted that. I had been allowed to pick out Beowulf at the pound. And for a small while the puppy was dependent and awkward and cute enough to make me forget about the fact that I really longed for a baby brother or sister, or a foster child, or even a neighbor close to my age. I had promised to raise a second child if Mom would just go through the motions of birth. But that was a stale argument. The last time I had asked her, she couldn't consider a baby because she was starting a second career. She had begun classes at the Institute of Ecosystems Studies.

"Good. You're well-qualified for that," Father had said. (Mother was a middle school social studies teacher.) She had just laughed, though. The next week she began potting perennials and planning the re-landscaping of our property. She was going to learn to drive a tractor. But that was last year.

"I'm sure your daughter is well-intentioned, but, Mrs. Hill, for the dog's correct integration into your household, every-one, including your husband, must be committed to the healthy development of this animal."

At that moment I heard my father in the kitchen emptying the last dregs of coffee into a cup and snapping open the morning paper. Probably the editorial section. Mom heard him, too. Her voice lowered an octave. "Well, I see no problem," she said.

"The dog will come with me for ten days, and—using a variable schedule of positive reinforcement—I will teach the dog the basic behaviors. After the dog's initial socialization, I will need to meet every other day with all of you in your home, Mrs. Hill, to review the dog's interaction with the family."

I pictured my father and Leonard Roth. My father would not like Leonard Roth telling him how to establish a meaningful relationship with a dog. I remembered my father's response when my mother had wanted him to go to a marriage counselor with her after he moved into the studio. Mom said they needed to learn "to communicate." He was cooking breakfast. "That's intelligent, Linda. Pay someone to tell us to talk to each other. Pay him to eavesdrop while you repeat the same complaints I can hear for free."

Later that night I had tried to cheer up Mother by baking a carrot-orange cake. While I was shredding the carrots in the blender, she sat at the table drinking tea and told me how carotene was transformed to Vitamin A in the liver. But after the cake came out of the oven, she said she wanted to go to bed with a new book from Eleanor. "It's about loving yourself," she explained as she stabbed a moist crumb flaking off her sliver of cake and put it to her lips. She read me a few passages and said that it might even be a good book for me to read when I became a teenager. "That's an extremely difficult time for so many young people," she had said sadly as she left for bed.

My father smiled and swung open the door to the studio when he saw me standing there with the piece of carrot-orange cake. I had placed a dessert fork on the plate at exactly the same angle it had been in the glossy magazine ad with the recipe. "Mom and I made it for you," I told him. "It's a good source of vitamin A."

But my father never agreed to go to a counselor, and I knew that if my father didn't go for the people therapist, he was never going to go for the dog therapist. For just a moment, I felt my

16

shoulder blades sag with relief. Oh good. Maybe Leonard Roth wouldn't get the job. I didn't like the dog psychologist or his dog robot who had my name.

I watched my mother plotting frantically to cross this huge mountain pass between the endless scoring of heels and Beowulf's socialization. "But surely my daughter and I...I mean my husband's very busy. Isn't there a compromise?" Mother's voice had become a whisper, giant snowdrifts piling against it.

The dog psychologist leaned forward, his voice smooth as butterscotch. "This is a family project, Mrs. Hill. Its success depends on the participation of everyone with whom the animal interacts."

"So. How do we learn the commands?" my mother asked Leonard Roth. I groaned. She was going to hire a shrink for my dog.

The dog psychologist smiled for the first time, his black therapist's stare burning through my mother's hesitation.

Then Mother smiled too, her entire frame relaxing. She took a sip of tea. "So Leonard, how did you ever get into this business? You're so sensitive and knowledgeable that I'm surprised you're not working with people instead of dogs." She leaned back into the couch again and hugged her knees to her chest. I imagined my father in the kitchen listening to the lilt in her voice.

Leonard Roth had, in fact, begun working with human beings. He had worked with emotionally disturbed children in Taos, New Mexico, for seven years. But, he explained, "I was not making enough money for what I do." He had used dogs as tools for treating the children and that is where he learned how to socialize a dog. Then, after he had socialized all the dogs in Taos for a lot of money, making what he was worth, he had brought his talents East to our community. My mother was agreeing, her microcosmic, acu-yoga voice ebbing and flowing, that it is essential for each person to feel that his or her talents are receiving adequate appreciation.

Soon Violet and Leonard were socializing, and Melville, Beowulf, and I were not feeling much like part of the pack.

They didn't even notice when I took the dogs and slipped outside. I wanted to try swinging Beowulf by her neck. As I passed through the kitchen, I could see my father's eyebrows were furrowed and a black fog had settled over his shoulders. He turned a page of the paper without looking at it. The dog psychologist had been at our house for over an hour.

When I was growing up, my father thought my mother was funny. Beowulf would have had no trouble comprehending the hierarchy in our cave then as the baton passed smoothly back and forth with the regularity of a metronome. Once, when Mom had driven on a flat tire for two days and the whole wheel on her car had to be replaced with money my father was saving to buy a new lawn mower, she finally asked him why he hadn't gotten angry. "Come on," she said, "act like you're supposed to. Get mad."

"Linda," he said, "I've been trying for ten years to get you to close the cupboard doors, to watch the oil light and tire treads on your car, and to behave. I wash my hands of the whole thing." The light sparkle of their laughter echoed through the kitchen.

I can't remember exactly when my mother and father locked horns. It happened soon after Linda became "Violet" and joined a book club. She kept wanting my father to "talk to her" more. "Does that mean you're going to listen?" he said. But this time she didn't laugh. When my mother first brought home books by the Leonard Roths of the world, my father teased her about the "hot tub verbiage," but gradually he began spending more time working on the property. The more wood he chopped, the more classes Mother took. I had a feeling that a therapist for the dog represented the final chop of the ax.

I was sitting in the grass with the rolling, twisting puppy when Leonard Roth and Mother came out into the driveway. She was saying, "Well, when could we begin?"

"Any time after Tuesday will be fine," Leonard Roth was saying, as he placed one foot on the running board of his truck. "You do know that this is very expensive, Mrs. Hill." I had no idea how Mother planned to jump that hurdle. My father's aversion to spending money surpassed even his dislike for therapists. Last year she told Father that she bought all of the tools for her landscaping project "on sale." When she realized I heard her, she pulled me aside. "Now that's not really a lie. It all works out in the end, Honey. Remember how I replaced the broken blender last week at that garage sale with a perfectly good one for $1.50. You see?"

18

"I have been warned. I have some money set aside," said my mother to Leonard Roth.

"The price—irrelevant of how long this takes—for the complete social integration of the animal into your household is $1,000."

My mother's eyes became instantly glossy. "My God. I had prepared myself for even $200. I've gotten you out here for all this time, but…I didn't suspect…I just couldn't justify—not with…. You don't have a short course for $200?" she finished, her voice a whisper from the bottom of a well.

Leonard Roth's eyes sparked like onyx. "A dog is a lifelong investment. Some people feel the psychological comfort of their dog and the carefully orchestrated interaction with an animal every day for the lifetime of that animal is valuable."

"I'm just not sure. I'll have to call you, but…I'm sorry." Mother was staring at Leonard Roth's shoulder as she spoke. As he swung into the cab of his red truck, the dog psychologist told my mother to call him next week "if you change your mind, Mrs Hill." We watched as the dog psychologist's truck rounded the corner out of sight. Greta, the dog with my name, was standing at attention in the back of the truck.

I knew my mother's expression. It was all going to be my father's fault. Violet slumped into a chair at the kitchen table. "It costs about $500," she told my father. She then began to scatter the phrases "poor animals," "resocialization," "the pack," "the studio," "dominant behavior," "watchdog," and "heel scoring" into the air.

Finally my father looked up. "Do you mean, Linda, that that man was willing to train you, Greta, and Beowulf for only $500? Get him back here. I'll break into the washing machine money."

Through the screen door, I saw my mother look at him with January in her eyes, her lips stretched tight. The seasons changed forever in our house that day. I wanted her to laugh like she used to when my father teased her.

Suddenly I wished I were wearing a sweater, but I didn't want to go into the house. I wrapped my skinny, bare arms around the puppy and carried the squirming animal to my secret thinking place in the woods behind the house. Beowulf gnawed on my dungaree leg and then, with her giant paws, stalked and crushed a brown-trimmed leaf that had flipped across our path. I didn't have any desire to hang her by the neck. I thought about the dog with my name. At that moment I knew that even if I baked 100 carrot-orange cakes for my father or cashed in my college savings bonds from Grandma Janice and paid $1000 to resocialize Beowulf, no one thing—not a class in yoga, or traditional values, or love, or a twelve-week-old Lab mix who would fight a garbage truck to save our home—could protect us.

"Beowulf," I said, "let's hike the back trail." We set off together, hoping to make the best of the last day of autumn and fearful of winter.

The Little Blonde

Gene Patterson

It was an older woman, an actress wise in the ways of men, who observed and exposed my weakness. For some time I had owned and driven a vintage Mercedes automobile, a sporty convertible whose striking beauty drew admiring attention on the highways. The hours I spent on its grooming and care were a pleasurable pastime that was oddly tinged with guilt.

The actress knew a loving look when she saw one. One day, watching as I tinkered with the fog lamps, she spoke pointedly to my wife.

"Look at him—that's his 'little blonde,'" I heard her say. My wife laughed, but I knew I blushed.

In bed that night I admitted to myself that she had touched on the truth. I was infatuated with the Mercedes. Its sleek, classic lines became tempting sensuality in my inflamed mind. And it had happened before, too. Other, long-ago cars flirted through my drowsiness, as old sweethearts sometimes invade our dreams. In a half-sleep, I felt myself smiling. Casanova in his waning days must have smiled such a smile as he riffled through the pages of his little black book. My own memories were filled with four-wheeled loves: charmers whose amusing anomalies, surprising caprices, and hidden delights made them unforgettable.

Casanova, it is said, attended love's kindergarten tenderly tutored by his nursemaid. At an age when many children still cling to their sleepy blankets for self-gratification, I was watching my teenage brother engage with his Model T Ford in our farmyard among the clutter of Mama's chickens, when I felt the first stirrings of auto fetishism.

Russell had become a sophisticated lover of cars. He leaned over the Model T and stroked its black enamel with affectionate familiarity. (Henry Ford had decreed that the customer could have "any color he wants as long as it's black.") Firmly, knowingly, Russell lifted the engine cover. Gently he wiped moisture from the spark plugs; his head and shoulders disappeared as he felt for a possible radiator leak. Emerging with a pleased look he closed the hood and reached inside the car to a switch on the coil box. With a practiced gesture he raised the spark lever on the left of the steering column and lowered the opposite throttle control.

Standing back a few respectful steps with my little red wagon I kept hoping he would say "Run get me the Stillson wrench on my dresser" or otherwise include me in the affair. But he walked up front for the ceremonial starting of the car. Pulling the projecting loop of the choke wire with his left hand, he reached down with his right for the crank that hung below the radiator. He pulled it up sharply, then again, and once more without result.

He was interrupted by a cheeky rooster that flew up in the car, crowed impudently and left his mark on the back of the driver's seat. Swearing, my brother grabbed off his hat and flung it at the rooster, who flapped down squawking.

Russell bent over again and spun the crank angrily. When the engine broke into faltering hiccups, he dashed back, advanced the spark and eased off the gas to quiet the uproar that was sending the chickens running for cover. Retrieving his cattleman's hat, he set it on at a rakish angle, then paused like Pygmalion admiring his success. From his shirt he took a muslin bag of Bull Durham. He shook the brown shreds into a cupped paper, rolled and moistened its edge with his tongue, and smartly lit a kitchen match with his thumbnail. As he slipped the Bull Durham back with its tag hanging out, he seemed to notice me for the first time, and grinned.

"Well, *Bol*ivar," he said—I didn't understand the nickname but it pleased me—"keep the home fires burning, and don't do anything I wouldn't do."

He turned to the palpitating flivver. Henry Ford, a frugal man, never gave the Model T touring car a driver's door. Instead he had traced a raised outline where the door wasn't. Ladies and older drivers slid across from the passenger's side. My brother chose an acrobatic approach, lifting his skinny butt over the non-door into the driver's seat, then jackknifing his long legs to let his cowboy boots follow him in.

Watching Russell get underway, I knew the ritual by heart; scrunched up in my little red wagon, I imitated every move he made.

As he released the hand lever at his side, the clutch pedal rose against his left foot. Pressing it back down to the floor to start off in low gear, he opened the steering wheel gas throttle, gaining speed. Rolling along briskly, he eased the clutch pedal halfway back to neutral, relaxed the throttle, then raised his foot from the clutch. As the car shuddered into high gear, he gave it the gas again. Jolting down the road, he bent over the coilbox to switch a lever from "Battery" to "Magneto."

Ending my impersonation, I twisted one last imaginary lever on the wagon. As Russell and the Model T rumbled over the distant cattle guard I waved in vain hope of being noticed again. Mama's hens were cautiously regrouping and the dust cloud had faded across the pasture before I went back to pulling my wagon, making a loud "Rrrr!" noise, filled with yearning and resolve.

When I reached seven my father let me guide his car (standing, to reach the controls) along the sandy ruts of our road. By the time I was ten he was sitting by my side while I drove on the highway. That was not unusual in the 1920s. Country kids learned to handle a car almost as soon as they rode a horse, and driving licenses, required by some Eastern states, were considered bureaucratic folderol by Texas lawmakers.

The fall after I was thirteen nobody had time to drive me to school. Daddy and Russell had cut down an over-the-hill Dodge touring car to make an open pickup truck for bringing cow feed home and hauling cream to the train. It was turned over to me. In my sleep, Mama said, I kept murmuring "my car." I painted my first love a rich green and lettered a sign on the door for a budding business venture: selling Crosley radios and a unique kerosene refrigerator. "CROSLEY ICYBALL" the sign read.

Always alert, Cousin Emert publicized my initiative. "Here comes old Icyballs!" he would call across the schoolyard whenever I drove up. Snickers and giggles trailed us all over town. Even my druggist friend Carl, who had taught me about radio, picked up the nickname and spread it among the locals at his soda fountain. But the Dodge and I would not be separated. For two school years my topless companion and I braved drenching cloudbursts and the raw chill of Texas winters in search of higher education. We might never have parted but for the siren call of the city and my first job.

Living away up north in San Antonio I was loyal for a long while to the memory of the Dodge, as I walked to work and tramped alone to the movies. At last, though, it became clear that I really needed a car of my own, and not just to drive around the city. I had a burning desire to *park* somewhere. The source of my stress was blue-eyed and filed papers in the radio station where I worked. A young announcer was already dazzling her with his cheap show biz charm; studio operators were conspicuously short of glamour. If I owned a car, I reasoned, I could install a radio in it (car radios were not yet in general use) and—driving to some romantic spot—"have my way," whatever that meant, with the maiden.

An engineer at the WOAI transmitter was sorrowful about selling his Essex car to a junk dealer. "It runs real good," he told me. "And if it won't start, you just use this big screwdriver."

I hesitated. Essex cars were the poor relatives of the Hudson motor car family, with a notorious peculiarity of design: an open flywheel whose works were exposed to mud and dirt. Besides, this little Essex had been neglected, perhaps even molested and abused in early life. But it had an appealing gamine allure that touched me. I circled it once, cautiously kicked a worn tire, and bought it for twenty dollars—a week's salary.

Ignoring a heavy rain that flooded the city streets, I drove away in high spirits. At the first stop sign the Essex answered the brakes like a circus performer, neatly spinning about to face the cars that had been following us. Somewhat at a loss, I returned up the street I had just come down, smiling at the perplexed drivers while making a note to humor the brakes at intersections thereafter.

Most times the car responded promptly. But at times the starter and transmission locked horns, so to speak. Then I had to hop out with the big screwdriver, slide under the running board, reach midway beneath the car, and pry the cogs of the flywheel loose. Then the car started willingly, though the nervous racing of its high-speed engine distressed timid

24

passersby. In no time I had a radio in the Essex (a Crosley 601 Bandbox from home, relic of my brief retailing phase) spouting tinny melodies to delight the young lady, and I was ready to compete with that air-headed announcer. Some offhand remarks about my new car radio and the date was cinched.

True, it was awkward, kneeling beside the car in my good pants to free the flywheel as her parents watched from their front porch. But once we drove away, I turned the radio on, and she was impressed. I was eager—perhaps too eager.

The radio was tuned to the station we both worked for—our station. "Let's drive out into the country and sit and, well, sort of listen to music," I ventured. But my left eyelid was twitching uncontrollably and something was happening to the casual voice I had rehearsed. The orchestra was playing "Stardust." My giddiness was intense.

Then the song came to an end and the unctuous voice of my competition spoke. Over my radio. Cutting in on my date.

"This is Corwin Riddell speaking," he intoned.

"Dumb name." I complained.

"Shh." She was *listening* to that nincompoop!

"From the starlit Roof of the Gunter Hotel in the heart of San Antonio, you're hearing the delightful dance music of Herman Waldman and his Brunswick recording orchestra..."

She looked at me coquettishly for the first time ever. "Wouldn't it be fun to drive down there and surprise Corwin?"

I would sooner have died than take her to visit Corwin Riddell. The only time I had ever been to the Gunter Roof Garden was to install a microphone; the mere mention of dancing brought on a cold sweat, and I only had a dollar and seventy-nine cents till payday.

Now Waldman's band was playing "Lazy River," a catchy arrangement where the whole band sang. But the wind was out of my sails. "Too late," I told her, heavily. "The show is nearly over." I turned off the radio, with the excuse that my battery was running low. In a certain sense, it was. Forlornly, I drove her to a miniature golf course in Brackenridge Park. She was not amused. At the third hole she excused herself, left for a long time while I died, then returned saying she was not well and would like to go home.

Sadly, I took the radio from the car and back to my room at the YMCA, and a scant month later Corwin Riddell lost the fickle maiden to a handsome car salesman. Corwin and I got to be pretty good friends during lonely winter evenings at work with not much to do but report line trouble back to NBC New York and make station breaks between the A & P Gypsies and the Clicquot Club Eskimos. For solace I tinkered with the car, my lady Essex.

Happily, I was soon joined by Louis, my boyhood mentor and friend, drawn like me to the city lights. Our club and cultural center was the Brooks Sandwich Shop, one of whose waiters invited us to share his ample room in Mrs. Murphy's boardinghouse up on Main Avenue.

In our new home we found conviviality quite different from the YMCA's. A colorful group gathered daily around Mrs. Murphy's breakfast table. There was her policeman son, Spud, who moonlighted in bootlegging, and his sister, who lounged by day in her dressing gown and left in glad rags at dusk. Among other boarders were WOAI's senior announcer and his dark-haired, voluptuous wife. One afternoon the lady asked me to her room. There she confided that her husband was cheating, and sought my comfort. I mumbled deep concern and fled.

Yes, folks were sociable *chez* Murphy. Evenings, there was entertainment beneath my window, where pleasure-loving gourmets parked at a drive-in hamburger place for Amos 'n' Andy's ten o'clock radio show. I got used to dozing off while Andy rumbled and Amos voiced high-pitched dismay and the late snackers guffawed in their automobiles.

One morning at daybreak I awoke to a loud knocking. I imagined that Louis or the waiter had infringed a house rule, but since they pretended to be sleeping, I answered the door. It was a large uniformed policeman, and it was me he was after, or someone with my name.

"You own a 1925 Essex?" he demanded. I said yessir, it was right downstairs.

"Put on your pants and bring your keys and come with me," he said, with what for a policeman seemed like a pretty funny look. Uneasy, I followed him out Mrs. Murphy's door. The gently sloping street was empty. My car was gone.

"What happened?" I asked.

"Look down there," the cop said, pointing. In the distance my lady Essex sat comfortably in the exact center of an intersection. Sometime in the night, I suppose, her weary hand-brake relaxed and a block and a half later she ended astride an important crossing. The cop had been waking people for half an hour to find the owner, but he was very decent about it.

"You better get that jalopy out of there, kid," he said. "Somebody might spoil its good looks. And listen, when you park on a hill, crimp the wheels to the curb, will ya?"

I thanked him warmly, though "kid" hurt. In the flat, sandy country I came from, cars couldn't roll away, but he didn't have to know that. I hotfooted it down to the car, shirttail and shoestrings flapping, and she started without the screwdriver.

During the lean years I shared with my lady Essex, she never ducked a challenge, though I worried about her increasing frailty. So I hesitated when a friend asked me to drive one weekend to Houston, two hundred miles away. Frank was a laid-off railroad telegrapher who hoped for a job in the radio station where a mutual friend was already riding out the hard times. "We can visit with Harold and I'll buy the gas," he proposed. Overhearing, another friend asked if we'd bring home his father, also an old-time telegrapher, who was stranded in Houston.

The distance must have tried my aging Lady, but the trip was made serenely. In Houston we saw Harold, and after a weekend of pleasure, loaded on the old telegraph man, noting that he was already well-loaded for the trip back.

At sundown we started for San Antonio, but a few miles out my loyal transportation became cranky and irritable. Old Dad was curled up and snoring even before we cleared the city limits. It may in fact have been his alcohol fumes that started the cough in the engine. Distressed, I pulled off the highway into a shed claiming to be a garage. The resident mechanic tinkered for an hour before he finally shrugged and asked for three dollars.

There wasn't anything like three dollars among us. Frank and I had spent our weekend money on riotous living and gasoline, and there was no sense trying to wake up the impecunious drunk in the back. So I took off my Illinois watch and left it for security, thinking guiltily of my parents who had given it to me. We drove off into the darkening night, but something was still wrong: the headlights were fast getting dimmer. Frank lit a match and reported that the generator was not charging the battery. Once the car stopped it could never start on its own again. I slowed to a crawl and turned off the failing lights.

A dark moment later the clear night brought out the faint outline of the road for my straining eyes. As we rolled along in obscurity, anonymous and unheralded, a wild sense of freedom surged in me. Frank, who sang quite badly, began crooning "Under a Texas Moon." At first I turned on the dull headlamps briefly to warn each approaching car, but this prompted such a startled honking that I soon gave up on the lights and took to steering off the road each time one flashed past. It was a rough choice because of the hidden bumps and potholes at roadside.

A hard jolt awoke the old man in the back and he groaned. Then he leaned forward, his hundred-proof breath warming the back of my neck—and let out a yelp of fright.

"Oh, Lord Jesus! Boys, I've gone blind!" he cried out. Frank soothed him, explaining that our lights were turned off by necessity, and his relief was touching. "God A'mighty, that had me worried. Feller never knows what he's drinkin' nowadays. Thank you, thank you!" He groped in the dark for his bottle to steady his nerves.

The night wore on as the moon moved over my shoulder toward San Antonio. Where we were was uncertain; if there were road signs they could not be read. My eyes burned from blinking back the dimness. We were lonely. In the blinding flash of headlights were we glimpsed as a dark shape humping along the road's edge? Or worse, unseen? Small talk lagged, then ended, while time and space mingled mysteriously. Our ghost ship, riding an asphalt ocean, bore three glum spirits on through an alien, invisible world.

In short, it was a long night. As the stars faded, my lady Essex labored ever harder. Finally we made out a landmark near San Antonio where the road dropped sharply to cross a narrow bridge. On the far slope we lost momentum. Near the top the Essex chugged her last, sighed—and died.

Dismounting in the dismal gray, I sized up the road behind us. Maybe the engine would revive if I rolled *backward* down the hill. I routed the others out, took another fearful look at the bridge below, and gave Frank a last message for my mother. Then I released the brake for my retrograde dash of death.

But the worn-out Essex sat motionless. I asked Frank and the old man for a push backwards. With wheels locked, the car refused to stir. "Please stop trying," she seemed to say. "I'm so tired. Go on without me."

"Someone has to go find a phone and call for help," I said. But all at once Frank's stomach was hurting and the old man, resting on a rock, had dozed off. In the pale dawn I trudged to a distant farmhouse, braved two unreasonably watchful dogs, and convinced the suspicious farmer that I needed to use his phone. "Even a criminal gets to make one call," I reminded him. The person I called was my hometown friend Louis.

It tests a friendship to be awakened at daybreak and led to the bedroom phone of an irate landlady, there to be asked to drive miles to rescue a bedraggled bunch of travelers. Louis passed the test with hilarious laughter. It was the sweetest music I ever heard. He reached us at sunrise, still laughing.

"No wonder it won't roll downhill!" he chuckled. He showed us that the leaf spring by the rear wheel had broken on one of those fearful potholes. That had pulled the brake rod tight, forcing the abused automobile to toil against odds all night.

Louis brought us home, and on payday I redeemed my watch. But I was immature and lacking character: unable to face repairing all her worn-out parts, I left my lady Essex where she was and never went back.

On the rebound I flung myself into a stupid affair with a giddy little Durant coupé. This lasted only until my work took me to a northern city. There I met and (with the generous loan of my landlady's Studebaker) courted the girl who became my wife. That was the happy, wholesome side of life. But for someone weaned on a carburetor, those city years were a lean mixture, a nickel-and-dime interim of dreary streetcars, buses and the IRT subway; and Manhattan with wartime driving restrictions was a vehicular desert whose empty parking spaces yawned to taunt non-owners. Even after eventual peace my craving for the joys of internal combustion was thwarted by other family needs.

Throughout the long car-less years, I had ogled the great European automobiles on our Greenwich Village streets and lusted after them. But it was much later before I could even imagine one could be mine. At long last I heard from my German connection, a Hamburg entrepreneur of previously-owned automobiles. "I have the car you want," he wrote, and described my fondest hope, a 1960 Mercedes 220 SE cabriolet in pastel blue. He was sure we were meant for each other.

There was never a doubt. I arranged passage to Hamburg and met the dealer at his car lot. There in a sea of Mercedeses of all varieties and ages sat my dreamboat, my "little blonde."

"Lili Marlene!" I breathed. The dealer may have been short on romance, but he knew how to sell a car. He turned to leave us.

I called after him. "Is it all right if I get in?" Lili was tempting, all fragrant leather and zebrawood panelling and chrome and Blaupunkt radio and sky-blue, aristocratic elegance.

"*Ach, ja*, chust get acquainted," he replied. I opened the handsomely fitted door, slid behind the wheel, looked along the massive hood at the three-pointed star that twinkled ahead. "He was right," I exulted. "We *are* made for each other!"

The dealer came back with a bright-faced youngster. Would I like to take a ride? Of course I would, but I was too timid to drive, so I moved into the passenger's seat. The lad shook hands and took over.

Lili's engine roared with power. She shot out of the car lot like a frightened doe, opening up a path in the crowded streets among the startled Hamburgers. "Do we have some sort of official license?" I asked my cheery driver. He smiled back at my white knuckles. "*Ach, nein*. But people recognize a serious driver." Fifteen thrill-packed minutes later the demonstration ended and he helped me into the dealer's office, where a few simple exercises unclenched my fist so that a check could be written.

Although Lili Marlene seemed perfect to me just as she was, she needed new headlamps to get her U.S. visa. By sundown they were installed and we were headed toward Switzerland on the infamous Autobahn. Motorists—I took them to be dropouts from the Bader-Meinhof gang—raged past, trying to force Lili from the highway, but she resisted fiercely, roaring back at the mannerless Teutons.

When dusk fell I switched on the new lights. To my dismay they glared back from the windshields of oncoming cars and drew angry flashing from the short-fused German motorists. I tried to drive on with only the parking lights, but this brought on even more furious flashing and honking. Five thousand miles and fifty years away from my youth, the crisis of my last night with the Essex threatened to repeat itself. Exhausted, Lili and I pulled up at a roadside *hofbrau* and spent the night. The rest of the journey to Basel was made by daylight. There we met my wife and the deviant headlights were set straight.

As we grew better acquainted, other chinks in Lili's armor appeared. In Geneva a Mercedes master mechanic installed shock absorbers and autographed an impressive bill bearing his portrait. An hour later, climbing the French mountains, I casually shifted out of first gear—and nothing happened. Lili kept moving on sedately, ignoring the stick shift. No other gear, not even reverse, responded. When a wide enough place appeared, we turned around gingerly and crept back fifteen kilometers in first gear to a village mechanic. Though he was harried and overworked, he seemed touched by Lili's story.

"Back her up—uh no!—make a circle and drive in," he said. An hour later he had replaced the broken linkage and sent us on our way.

As our trip ended it was agreed Lili would precede us by sea. The young son of a Parisian friend was eager to take her to the ship in Le Havre. (We learned later that they spent that last night together on the dock!)

When the ship reached Brooklyn harbor I was there to meet my "little blonde." As expected, she drew admiring glances and whistles from Americans wherever she went. At that time she still seemed youthful, a distinguished beauty whose classic charm never dimmed during our years together.

Lili's aristocratic manner, her proud three-pointed star, her purring motor and easy grace brought her driver undeserved esteem, and I took delight in the reflected glory. Parked in Greenwich Village, she dignified the entire neighborhood. I was kept busy answering polite questions about her origin. Weekend visits to the Catskills became promenades permitting less fortunate car owners to pay homage.

I cannot be forgiven for leaving her during two years when my wife and I were obliged to be out of the country. A fascinated associate had asked to keep her while we were away and "just drive her down to the beach to keep her in condition." But when we returned it was clear that she had suffered from our absence. We took her to leading specialists in Manhattan; then, with failing hope, to clinics in Montclair, Englewood,

Albany, and Poughkeepsie.

The end seemed near when we reached an upstate New York sanatorium that had been recommended. A longhair in soiled coveralls eyed her, not with the deference she merited, but in coarse amusement. "Gee, that's an old one, ain't it?" he crowed.

I took her away at once, but her spirit was crushed. That spring she was placed for repairs with a sort of folk-hero practitioner in a distant city, who worked over her throughout the summer. At Labor Day he called.

"Better come for her," he said in flat, measured tones. "And treat her gently." His voice softened. "Perhaps your mountain air will help."

During this somber time of decision a phone call came from our daughter. She spoke tactfully. The school was having an auction. For the sake of the children, would we consider offering Lili?

Realizing that she needed care only a wealthy family could afford, we faced the inevitable. "It would be the best for Lili," my wife assured me.

On the morning of the auction, she still shone heartbreakingly beautiful. The symptoms of her age were erased as we rode together one last time. We knew the fortunate bidder, a well-to-do physician, who would give Lili the luxury and ease she needed.

Since that parting, my lifelong obsession with flashing spokes and purring motors has mellowed to a gentle yearning. I am older now. Passion's lamp burns low.

And yet—and yet. Ignoring the trade deficit a while ago, we opened home and heart to a neat and supple, responsive girl-car from the Orient. Mindful of envious neighbors and their lurking chauvinism, I must disguise the tenderness she arouses in me.

Of course, the "little blonde" is always in my heart. But in the long night of my autumn, it is not Lili Marlene's gleaming metal and perfumed leather that sends fantasy soaring on crippled wings. What haunts me is the dream of a dawn—one morning in the old, old past. Bluebonnets blanketing a Texas hill, a narrow bridge below. And by the road, now sweetly wreathed in honeysuckle vines—my lady Essex! Waiting for her faithless lover's return.

A Stranger

Mary Leonard

It bothers me that I haven't seen or heard him. His car's out front but there hasn't been any evidence of him for at least two days, not that I was consciously counting. It just seems strange. Usually if I'm at the kitchen sink, he'll be across the way fiddling with the shade on his window, or else I'll notice him clipping the hedge that separates the twelve feet between our properties. In my backyard, I'm not aware of neighbors. On my front porch, I can hear Mr. Morris talking on the phone. At least I always thought he was talking on the phone.

Mr. Morris was a shadow. I'd try to relax on my porch, fitting in bits and pieces for the *Times* crossword puzzle, when I would become aware of an annoying grating on the street. Mr. Morris would be raking the few dried leaves that cluttered the curb. Or sometimes, I felt he was a voyeur. My husband would startle me in the kitchen, grabbing me from behind, and Mr. Morris would be at his window, watching.

My fourteen-year-old, Tom, claimed that Mr. Morris mowed his lawn every day, and scraped and repainted his house every summer. Looking at his house now makes me think of the weathered and patchy skin of the elderly. From a distance, the surface appears white and smooth. Up close, it tells stories. I'm 41. Twenty years ago, no one could have told me that my own skin would wrinkle. But Mr. Morris and his house weren't reminders of aging. No, another memory. I guess I've wanted to repress that memory, or move my mind back, before the years of my father's illness, to a time when Dad was young and I was a kid. In the fifties, before the vacant lot became yet another new house in my childhood suburban neighborhood, Dad taught me how to play ball. He pitched to me underhand, gave me explicit advice about my batting, but mostly we played in silence. Those were the years before softball leagues for girls, so "The Jean Leary Gang," as we were called, played in the Annunciation School parking lot. I wore a pair of prescription sunglasses, wheedled out of my mother, just for that purpose, and a red, white, and blue striped shirt that became my baseball uniform. I was good. Once I even hit a home run.

So when I pushed my memories, they would focus on my father in action. Saturdays spent paddling in inner tubes at Bayville, or August spent battling the waves at the "Joisey" shore. Or eating. I remember dinners in Patricia Murphy's pastel rooms, cute names like "The Billowy Ballroom," or when I was older, Friday nights at the Red Coach Grill. I ate what he ate—steamed lobster, raw clams, the catch-of-the-day. And drinking. We moved from Manhattans to Martinis to Dewars-on-the-rocks.

After I was married, he would arrive with his toolbox and repair faulty doorknobs and squeaky hinges. When I was eight months pregnant with my son, we bought this house and I became obsessed with painting the living room before my due date. My parents came up to help. I pulled my swollen body around the periphery to paint the woodwork. Mom was only 64 then, so Dad must have just turned 70.

We taped the windows to protect the glass, but it took so long to paint, that the masking tape baked in the July sun. It couldn't just be peeled off; it had to be scraped. It was frustrating for me to be so young and so incapable of mobility and control. I cried. My seventy-year-old father scraped the tape off the windows without one "shit" or "How could you be so stupid!" While the rest of us lounged on the porch, he spent the entire evening meticuously using a razor blade to clean those windows.

Today I'm trying to lounge on the porch, but I can't because I miss the sounds of sweeping and scraping. The neighborhood is quiet, too quiet. Mr. Morris usually works every day, sometimes listening to the Mets. In the early years of our move, we were neighborly toward Mr. Morris, engaging in pleasant chats about keeping bees and life on his mother's farm. One winter though, the fence that separated the back half of our properties collapsed. In the spring, I hired a young carpenter to replace the posts and put up a new fence. In the process, he muddied Mr. Morris's lawn.

"I can't see the property marker. If he puts the fence there,

34

the marker will be..." Mr. Morris whined.

My husband was trying to explain that the carpenter wasn't finished yet, that he would tidy up, that the property marker would be seen. His reasonable voice sounded loud and determined. He kept repeating logical answers to the plaintive plea of Mr. Morris's obsessions.

"The marker will be cleared as soon as the fence is up."

Mr. Morris raised his voice, "My grass is ruined, buried under the mud, that's my property buried under the mud."

My husband lost his cool and yelled at Mr. Morris, vowing never to speak to him again. It was difficult to avoid someone who lived only twelve feet away, but Mr. Morris helped by running inside every time he saw us. I still caught him peeking through the shade, but most of the time I heard him, talking on the phone. His voice was loud, much louder than that day in the driveway. He was complaining about the fence incident to someone who would listen. From my upstairs bathroom, I caught phrases: "grass ruined," "the marker is lost." At least he's getting out his anger, I thought. But one day, when I was clipping our side of the hedge early in the morning, I peeked in his open window. He was staring at a framed photograph, focusing his frustrations at the image. There was no phone. Through imaginary wires, he was chatting with the only person he was ever close to—his dead mother.

The scene did not shock me. I accepted his idiosyncrasy, deep down remembering my father's own mind-wanderings to childhood summers in Rhode Island, stickball in Hell's Kitchen, and to his own mother, always ill. I didn't make the connection then between Mr. Morris and my father. I only accepted Mr. Morris as my crazed but gentle neighbor. I made a point of waving or saying hello. I didn't want a neighborhood feud, carried on through generations, with neither side remembering why. Soon my husband resumed waving. We joked about Mr. Morris's obsession with his lawn, which was mostly crabgrass, or we laughed at his incessant circling of household chores, but mostly he was invisible, about as noticeable as the mailman.

It wasn't until this summer, while I was reading or working puzzles on the porch, aware of and moving with the neighborhood sounds—the clatter of house repair, the talk of birds and dogs, the melody of my new chimes—it wasn't until then, that I became haunted by his movement. It seemed as if, whenever I was caught in the rhythm of my book, or if I was about to discover a new thought, my mind would be pulled back by the sounds of clipping and scraping. Even now, while I'm writing, his sounds are jarring. I'm never interrupted by a barking dog or the sudden start of a chain saw, only Mr. Morris. Maybe it's like a stuck record. I can't move on, unless I pick up the needle.

We were living in this very same house when my mother began to call regularly to tell me about my father's bickerings with neighbors. Bickering wasn't odd for my father, except that now, once people crossed him, he erased them from his life. No reconciliation could occur. Dad would no longer speak to Dr. Cohen, after the doctor failed to be grateful for my father's weekly trek to the station to pick up the Sunday *Times*. Dr. Cohen simply commented, "This week the paper is missing the magazine."

"That no-good-son-of-a...," Dad fumed. "Let him go, every Sunday, what did he think, did he think I stole his paper." Mother placated him the best she could.

Then Dad refused to acknowledge Mrs. Reilly after her dog barked all night. He didn't tell her why. He just stopped saying hello on his morning walk.

Dad trimmed the hedges at the farthest edge of the backyard until only bare branches were showing. He let the part on the Smith's property go wild and then he wouldn't have to look at their "goddam pool."

Relatives, or friends from "the old days," would come to visit and, after an hour or two, Dad would retreat to a quiet room. Most of the oldtimers tolerated him. New acquaintances wound up asking Mom to lunch.

Dad had always been eccentric. As kids we knew the rules. To avoid traffic, we left on long trips before daybreak. We went out for the "Early Bird Special," not because of the price, but to avoid the crowds. We left gatherings before dark, we turned off the television promptly at ten, we never raised our voices, we told half-truths, and we wore blue, his favorite color, as often as we could. And we knew the consequences of breaking these unspoken rules—scorn, rejection, unforgivable anger. We knew. Why didn't others?

Dad had already alienated most of the neighborhood when he came upon a group of adolescents hanging out in a makeshift clubhouse near the station. They were probably smoking, drinking a six-pack of beer, basically harmless stuff. I don't know what Dad said, but I can imagine.

"Why don't you play ball?"

"We play with our balls, sometimes."

Dirty jokes were in the realm of pornography to Dad. He probably told them to beat it or he'd call the cops. They probably told him to go jerk off. The next time they saw Dad, he threatened them, but they got him instead. Mom found broken eggs all over her picture window.

Paranoia breeds isolation. Even in the early evening their house was quiet. As if they were both blind, they sat in the growing gloom, Mom, her eyes shut, her fingers flicking rosary beads, and Dad, filling in nonsense words for the crossword puzzles he couldn't see.

Once in a while, Mom would feed Dad information. "The Smiths called and want you to trim the back hedge."

"The Smiths?"

Mom wouldn't bother reminding him. He'd only forget by morning. She would glance at the glow-in-the-dark clock and start the before-bed ritual. Because Dad's feet ached on the hard bed, she wrapped them in gauze. Then she'd heat his milk and set three vanilla wafers on a plate. Sometimes the phone would ring. Some neighbor would complain about the Christmas decorations, now that it was May, or the way Dad tacked up too many chimes and bird feeders on the back porch. The sounds were driving them mad.

Mom would put the neighbors off, "I'll tell Alfred. He'll take care of it in the morning."

Dad would call her name and then make demands, endless demands. The pillow was too soft, the shade was too high, the air too warm. Mom patiently endured the necessary steps for them both to get some sleep.

I am dozing on the porch. A summery haze is shielding me from sounds and interruptions, except for one, a raking on the asphalt. Mr. Morris is back. He sees me, waves, and then he inches his way toward me.

"Were you visiting a friend?" I ask.

"My mother's farm needed tending."

"I didn't know you still owned the farm."

"My mother lives there." He leans back and forth on the

bottom step, a childlike preamble to a request.

"I want to cut the hedge down low. It's too high."

"Go ahead. Why not? It will give you something to do."

As soon as I said, "something to do," I wanted to bite my tongue. When Dad lapsed into the past, we tried to keep him busy. We bought him watercolor sets, easy-to-assemble bird feeders, electrical parts so he could redesign old lamps. The theory was that if we kept Dad occupied, he wouldn't fight with his neighbors. Mom finally took him to a specialist who de-emphasized the deterioration. "He knows Reagan's name. And how many people know the alternate routes from here to Long Island! Don't worry."

We did worry. We watched Dad hesitate in doorways, unable to decide which room to enter or where to sit. We listened to him ask, "What time is it?" so often that we took to posting on a blackboard near his seat: "The time is…" He wasn't a senile old man, pleasantly nodding on the sofa. His mind was gone; his body was healthy. He could still hike for miles, and when I would walk with him, he would lapse into childhood, summers crabbing on the Warren River, eels wrapping themselves around his arms. These stories didn't start, "I remember when," but were reenactments of moments or summaries of resentments, all told as if I weren't present.

"Mario lived with my Aunt Susan. He had a good life. My mother sent him to live in Warren and we were all jealous. Mario had all the milk he could drink, the cream on top in those days, and he didn't appreciate it."

I didn't remind Dad that milk was not a substitute for mother; he didn't want to be answered and he wasn't aware of my presence.

When we speak of a due date for birth, we are definite, but when we speak of death, we can only identify "six months before he died," afterwards. Six months before Dad died, he wanted to go home to his mother. That was the only home and relationship he remembered. All other family members eluded him. We'd introduce ourselves. "I'm your daughter, Ann. This is your grandson, Tom." During those six months of elusive identities, my sister died. On the way to the funeral, my mother and I rode in the back of the limo with Dad. We had been answering the question, "Who died?" so many times, that it became an absurd litany, a cruel reminder like a child's taunts.

He may have been journeying to the funeral of his oldest daughter, but he was now a boy conversing with his dead mother.

Before today, I hid those moments, but Mr. Morris is back. He's a reminder, like a leftover conversation, an irritant forcing me to pick up the needle and start the record again, this time in the middle. Starting over doesn't mean erasing, just realizing.

Mr. Morris is back and so is my father. I wish Dad could have told stories. I would like to have heard how he was almost drafted for a major league baseball team; but he was not a story teller, nor a man of words. When he was sick, he spoke his most lucid words right here on this porch, "I wish I had never been born." Dad was never philosophical, so what I think he meant to say was that he wished he were dead. Those words were not like the petulant whine of an adolescent, but the moment when a grown man realized that life was so difficult to end that maybe it should not have begun.

Mr. Morris is back. He's clipping the hedge. It's neat and trim. And I keep sitting here filling in words to a puzzle I can't complete. But I know this: Mr. Morris is a shadow I don't want to disappear. He's a reminder of what came before me and what could be.

What if I'm sitting on this porch someday, and I see a stranger emerging from my house. Will I say, "Who are you? What are you doing in my house?" And will he answer, "I am your son, Tom. Don't you remember me?"

Toy Soldiers

Maria Bauer

The boy sat on the edge of his cot, his clenched fists between his knees, and stared at his fort on the game table. For a moment he had the vision of smoke drifting out of its red turret the way it did when his father blew cigar smoke into it. It had looked so real then, even his toy soldiers had looked alive when his father positioned and commanded them into battle. But now all of them, the friendly and enemy soldiers, lay jumbled together and he didn't even care to straighten them out; they looked dead anyway.

It was no fun playing alone, but what else was there to do? Whenever he went to his mother's room—no matter how quietly so as not to disturb her—his aunt always sent him out, telling him "go play in your room," as though he could or wanted to play every time a grown-up told him to; like when he was told to go to sleep he knew that no matter how he'd try, he'd keep turning from one side to the other until he'd end up seeing monsters on his ceiling. And these days he couldn't even turn on the light when he was scared. There was no electricity, no gas, no coal. Why were things so much worse now that the war was finally over? Yet for four years everyone complained and said if only the war were over everything would be wonderful. Of course, everyone thought that the war would be won—every day there were reports about a victory here and a victory there—so no one could expect that the enemy would win and come, months later, all the way here to occupy Klagenfurt.

He wondered how things were before the war but he just couldn't remember. The only thing he did remember—and very clearly—was the first time he had seen his father in uniform. It was his 4th birthday and they were still living in Vienna. That day, many people—friends and relatives—kept walking into and out of their apartment, all talking loudly and seeming very excited. No one had paid any attention to him at all. But that evening Father had come to his room—so big and handsome in his light blue uniform with a broad black ring around his left sleeve—and he allowed him to touch everything: the course cloth of his uniform, the smart cap and visor and the shiny smooth stars on each side of his collar. Father didn't even get annoyed at him as he sometimes did when he kept asking, "why?" and "what's that?", but patiently explained everything: the silver stars showed that he was an officer, a lieutenant. And the black ring was a mourning band worn by all officers because Austria was in mourning for Archduke Franz Ferdinand and his wife Sophie, who had been murdered in Sarajevo. Yes, of course, those Serbian assassins would be punished—that's why Austria had to go to war. And, of course, Austria was going to win because Francis Joseph was a good emperor and Austria was a great country and God was on its side. And when Father kissed him good night he said: "You'll always remember that in 1914, the year of your 4th birthday, Austria went to war. It will only be a short war—more like a battle—and soon I'll be home again."

But the war had gone on and on and now that he was already 8 years old and the war was finally over, he didn't care anymore because his father would never be home again.

"Karli, don't you hear me," his aunt said, walking into his room. "Your mother is worse. You have to go down to the Army Hospital to get the doctor, Major Hoelzl..."

"All the way to the Army Hospital? But that's where the enemy is. And you said that Major Hoelzl is a prisoner."

"A prisoner of war, but they still let him work there and take care of his patients. So hurry up."

"But what if the enemy soldiers see me? You know what they do to children."

"Karli, you are a big boy now. You must be courageous for your mother. Now get going, quickly. You know the way—all the way down to the Stadttheater and then you turn right..."

Without waiting for her to finish, the boy ran out of the house. Kreuzberg Avenue was deserted and awfully quiet; the only sounds were the tap-tap of his shoes on the cobblestones and, occasionally, the screeching of a cat in the distance. Why was no one about? Were people afraid? It was not even dark yet and the enemy soldiers only occupied the buildings downtown. They never came up to the suburbs, even in daylight.

The boy hated to be out alone at dusk when the fog floated down from the mountains as though it would envelop him in its milky streaks. Passing the familiar houses behind their fenced front gardens, he slowed down when he reached the Hoffmann's villa, hoping that Ernst would see him and maybe go with him since they always walked together to and from school. But the Hoffmann house with its closed shutters looked silent and forbidding like all the others.

He wished he would meet someone he knew. Maybe the grocery store would still be open so that, at least, he could exchange greetings with Mr. Kramer. But when he reached it, it too was closed, even boarded up. Had Mr. Kramer closed his shop for good as he said he would because business was too hard now that the money has gone crazy? The boy knew what he meant because he used to help his mother carry groceries home from the store but, lately, he had to help her carry shopping bags of money to the store and each time there were fewer and fewer groceries to take home. And, a few days ago, just before Mother got ill, she had to take a suitcase filled with paper money to the store and all she returned with was a loaf of bread, a bottle of milk, and six potatoes.

The boy started running again—he still had so far to go and the sooner he brought Dr. Hoelzl back, the sooner his mother would get well. His aunt's words kept ringing in his head: "You must be courageous for your mother." Did that mean that his mother might die? No, of course not. After all, she only had the flu. But why did they call it the "Spanish flu" when so many Austrians were sick with it?

He wished he could say a prayer for Mother, but he couldn't—he couldn't ever pray again after what he had done. No, he didn't ever want to think of that horrible day—he had to push that memory away. He would try to think of something else, of good things that had happened to him. So he thought of that pastry shop in Vienna his father had taken him to before he left for the war. They were sitting together, just the two of them, on pretty gilded chairs at one of the round marble-topped tables eating *Indianerkrapfen*, those delicious pastry puffs covered with chocolate icing and bulging with whipped cream. "Eat it slowly," his father had said, "because you won't eat anything like that for a long time." And Father had been right—never since had he seen Indianerkrapfen or whipped cream or even butter anywhere.

And then he thought of other good times when Father was stationed in Bosnia and sent for his mother and him and all of them spent the summer together in Banja Luka, it was so much fun living on a real farm with all kinds of animals. Even when Father was not there, it was a wonderful place for playing war games, like pretending the chickens were enemies and chasing them with his toy gun until they all fled out of the courtyard. Once one of the chickens hid in that huge haystack and wouldn't come out no matter how he banged his toy gun against the hay. So he ran into the house, took the big black key off the hook in his father's office and threw it into the haystack. But that hadn't been a good idea—not only because it didn't make the chicken come out but because it was the key to the regiment's cash box. Father was terribly angry that night when he found out what had happened to it. Now the boy couldn't remember anymore how that spanking felt but he did remember how much fun it was to help the soldiers his father had summoned to take the whole haystack apart. The chicken soon ran out but it was a very long time until they found the key.

That first year in Klagenfurt was fun too. His mother and he had moved there because Father had to fight on the Italian Front and it was close enough for him to visit them at least once a month. The boy was six years old then and started going to school and afternoons he learned to swim in the lake nearby and there were always children his age to play with in the Kreuzberg gardens. It all seemed so peaceful then—only once he saw a real battle in the air. He was on the balcony when he heard the noise: a roaring sound in the sky and the commotion below on the street where people gathered and screamed that one of our planes was fighting an Italian. And then he saw, way up there over the mountains, two tiny planes gracefully flying in circles, over and under and around each other, like toy planes playing catch. He got so excited that he got his toy gun and kept shooting at what he thought was the enemy plane. Then, suddenly, one of the planes turned into a big ball of fire and disappeared behind the mountains. He knew right away that it was the enemy plane because the people on the street started acting like crazy, cheering and hugging each other like silly kids.

At the time war seemed like an exciting game; only occasionally he heard about someone who had been wounded or killed but somehow it never occurred to him that anything could happen to his father. Maybe because all these years he had said a prayer for him every single night—well not exactly every night because sometimes he had been too tired or forgot—but then he would always go to confession the next day and be really sorry and say the Lord's Prayer five times as the priest told him to so that God would forgive him. Even when Father was brought back to the Army Hospital, it didn't occur to him that he might die because he was told that the doctors would remove the bullet from his back and then he'd be all right. So every day he waited for his father to come home and when, a week later, he was told that the war was over he was so happy thinking that Father would never have to leave again. That's why that morning when they all came to his room with solemn faces—his mother and aunt and Dr. Hoelzl and the priest—he first didn't understand at all what they were trying to tell him. Only when the priest said "Your father is now with God" he knew. And he became so furious that he didn't know what he was doing. "I hate God," he heard himself scream and only later he remembered how he had pulled the crucifix from the wall and thrown it on the floor and stamped on it. And he couldn't remember at all what had happened afterwards—only that feeling for days like being caught in a horrible dream that he couldn't wake up from. And, of course, he didn't dare to go to confession—the sin was too big—God would never forgive him. He had insulted God, but hadn't God betrayed him and the Emperor? Or maybe there was no God at all?

He shook his head to get these thoughts out of his mind and looked up. Further down on the corner he finally saw the Stadttheater where he would turn right and then the Army Hospital would only be several hundred yards farther. It was now getting dark and the unlit towering street lights on both sides started to look like the monsters on his bedroom ceiling. He stopped to remove his left shoe because, with every step, it chafed a stinging blister that had developed on his heel. But just then he became aware of noises in the distance: the rumbling of a carriage, a voice yelling something in a foreign language, a dog barking. Now he was very frightened. He started running again as fast as he could, reached the corner, turned right—and stopped. A little farther up stood a cluster of enemy soldiers with fixed bayonets on their guns. He wanted to turn back but one of the soldiers had seen him, nudged his companion and pointed to him. Now another soldier started walking toward him and as he came nearer, the boy saw that it must be an officer because his uniform looked different and instead of a gun and bayonet he had a saber fastened to his hip. The boy stood still as if paralyzed as the officer came closer and closer and only lowered his eyes so as not to have to look in his face. Then he heard a voice speaking softly in a very strange accent: "Little boy, why are you out so late all by yourself?"

"I must talk to Major Hoelzl in the Army Hospital," the boy answered, much too loudly.

"Who is Major Hoelzl and why do you have to talk to him?"

"Because he is our doctor and my mother is ill."

"Then we must hurry," the officer said and shouted some orders to the soldiers who took off running. Then, reaching for the boy's hand, he said: "My soldiers will look for your doctor—so let's go together to meet him."

"I can go by myself," the boy said curtly, withdrawing his hand.

"No, you shouldn't walk alone in the dark. Don't be afraid of me—I won't hurt you. I have a little boy at home who is about you age—he even looks a bit like you, that same blonde hair. I haven't seen him for over 18 months—that's 540 days. You see, he and I both count the days. But now it won't be much longer, I expect all of us to be sent home soon..."

The officer kept talking but the boy, trying to keep a distance from him as they walked, stopped listening. He was still afraid because he had always been told that "one could never trust the enemy." This friendly talk had to be a trick and he wondered what would happen to him next.

They had barely reached the Army Hospital when Dr. Hoelzl came running out, clutching his big black bag, looking haggard and much less dashing in his white coat than he used to in his uniform. "Your mother?" he asked breathlessly and then, taking the boy's arm, "let's go quickly."

"No, Major," the officer said. "I cannot let you walk. I ordered a carriage that should be here any minute." And already an open horse-drawn carriage was pulling up next to them.

The boy, climbing in behind the major, was relieved to see that the Serbian soldier on the driver's seat carried neither gun nor bayonet. And he did not seem ferocious at all the way Serbian soldiers had always been pictured. He had neither beard nor moustache and looked very young as he listened intently to the Major pointing out the way to him. Briefly, when his eyes met the boy's he smiled, reminding the boy of his favorite teacher.

"I told the soldier to wait for you, Major," the officer said. "So please take your time, all night if necessary." And then, with a pat on the boy's head: "Goodbye, little boy. I'll be praying for your mother."

The soldier snapped his whip and the carriage took off. The boy leaned against the major's shoulder. His throat felt tight and scratchy—he couldn't understand why now, when everything was going to be all right, he felt like crying.

"Dr. Hoelzl," he said. "Why was that officer so nice?"

"Why not? Your father would have done the same thing." And then, angrily as though talking to himself, he added: "Finally people can start acting again like human beings, now that this idiotic war is finally over and..."

"Idiotic?" The word shocked the boy so that he was unable to listen any further as Dr. Hoelzl rambled on. That "Just War," that "Glorious War," as it always had been called was now "idiotic?"

As horse and carriage, with a rhythmical clatter, bumped through the night, the boy, looking past the soldier's shoulder, saw that the fog had dissolved, revealing a round moon suspended in a starlit sky. The familiar sight of the Kreuzberg and the Karawanken Mountains in the background now seemed different. He felt confused and lost.

He started to think about the world beyond these mountains—what its people were really like and whether they lived and thought like Austrians. That Serbian boy who looked like him—did he play the same games and, from the other side, see the same moon and the same stars? And for the first time the boy wondered whether that Italian pilot whose plane had exploded also had a wife and a son at home.

Disturbing thoughts kept crowding the boy's mind until the

carriage jolted to a stop. Without a word, the doctor hurried to his mother's bedside and then the boy again sat on the cot in his room. By the dim light of an oil lamp he listened intently to the subdued noises next door. The whispered murmurs went on and on and he fervently wished that someone would talk to him. Then, suddenly, he heard his mother's voice, loud and clear, and now he was sure that she would be well again. Soon he would be allowed to go to her room. He imagined himself sitting by her bed and her smiling at him and he started to rehearse how he would tell her his adventures.

But he couldn't go on when he realized that he couldn't tell her all that had happened to him. How could he possibly explain to her all these things he himself didn't understand—that suddenly seemed to change everything around him? It was all so confusing—he felt as though he had been gone for years and yet he had only left today, this afternoon. And he himself felt different too—there was this lump pressing down on his stomach but it wasn't the feeling of sadness that he knew because now he didn't feel like crying. He told himself that now all was well—he had managed to do everything he had been told to do and now his mother would be well again but these thoughts didn't make the lump any lighter. Why?

Though he ached from exhaustion, the boy would not yet go to bed. There was so much to think about, to figure out. Suddenly, with determination, he walked to his game table, picked up his toy soldiers and threw them, one by one, into the ashbin standing by the blue tiled stove. Then, with increasing anger, he took the turret off his fort, pulled its walls apart and, as he started throwing the metal pieces into the bin, he heard his aunt's voice: "Karli, you may come in to see your mother now." His heart pounding, he jumped onto his cot, pulled the blanket over his fully-clothed body and pretended to sleep.

The War Ever
Tara McCarthy

During a Wartime summer, my father made the mistake of moving us from our real home—a small green village of New York—to the gunmetal-gray city of Akron, where he went to work for a giant rubber-tire factory.

The Akron street was not a proper street at all: it was enormously wide and marked off *this* side from *that* side as definitively as a state border drawn on a map. The stern brick houses opposite us looked miles away. To find someone to play with, I could no longer dash across a little road or sit humming on the lawn, my jacks in a drawstring bag, bouncing a rubber ball nonchalantly to tempt a passing friend into a game. No, Akron was different: your mother had to call up the neighbor to find out whether it was convenient for the children to play, and then your mother had to walk you across the street, and then you had to call your mother when you were ready to come home so that she could come over and walk you back again. My mother could not do any of this walking, because her left leg was in a cast, so I could not even get across the street to check out likely-looking jacks aficionados.

Photographs of our time in Akron show me with as tragic a face as a well-fed six-year-old can muster. I was, I felt, in a prison, with only my invalid parent and my little sister and my great-aunt Inez and a maid named Jello for company. My dog had deserted me, dying on the sofa of the Pullman roomette as we crossed some dismal farmland on the way West.

My mother had broken her leg back in New York, slipping on the ice while walking my dog at dawn. "I was walking Honeybunch's sweet little Mickey," my mother said to my father's new friends as she looked at me wistfully. "I almost lost my leg, didn't I, Dan?"

"Yes, she almost lost her leg," my father agreed. "She was

48

very brave to make this trip."

"I did it for Dan," my mother said. "This was such an *opportunity* for him. I couldn't let something like almost losing my leg stand in the way of his work, or of the War Ever."

It was in almost losing her leg that my mother had acquired Jello and conjured up Aunt Inez from remote towns near her childhood home in North Carolina. They were to be our helpers, allied forces moved in to succor the wounded and take over the battle of running the house. And tattered troops they were! Jello was sixteen years old and so terrified by the city that she had to be cajoled into leaving the house even to empty the garbage. She wept constantly over a soldier named Francis who was fighting in Europe. Jello wept as she washed the stairs, wept as she made lunch, and wept as she showed me photos of Francis. Aunt Inez was in her eighties. She wore live birds in her hair—her parakeets Sweetie and Sillabub. She had, my mother explained, very kindly agreed to act as our housekeeper, a job which consisted mainly of ordering groceries over the phone.

"Yankees are so rude!" Aunt Inez always said when she hung up. When the groceries arrived, she would once again tell Jello how to make what became the culinary staples of our brief stay in Ohio—salmon casserole, apple Brown Betty, and pineapple upside-down cake.

"We had this last night, I think," my father would say, arriving for dinner nattily attired in his office clothes and looking handsome as usual, giving me a wink as he used to in the old days and looking pained as I pouted at him and turned away. I hated him then. He got *out* during the day, as he always had, and as I never did anymore. How could he move me to this dreadful place?

"I hate it here!" I usually managed to say at dinner. "There's no one to play with!"

"Maybe your Aunt Inez could walk you across the street to meet the neighbors," my father suggested.

"Mercy, I can't do that!" my Aunt Inez answered. "Yankees are too abrupt! Besides, this child has her little sister to play with."

"I hate her!" I said, watching clinically as my sister's face turned sad.

Sweetie and Sillabub fluttered in Aunt Inez's hair. She would

49

say "Blood is thicker than water," or "A bird in the hand is worth two in the bush," then ring the little crystal bell she had brought from Down South, summoning the sobbing Jello in to clear the plates.

"Oh, my land! I don't know what to do! I just don't know what to do," my mother exclaimed. "Why can't everyone just be *happy*?" Little tears would well up in her eyes, perfect little tears the sight of which made even Jello pause in her weeping.

After dinner, we would all move to our special places, moving in our special ways—my mother hobbling and grimacing into the living room to listen to "Mr. Keene, Tracer of Lost Persons," and resisting my father's offers of assistance, saying "No, I don't want to be a burden. Painful as this is, I'll do it on my own, thank you!"; Jello sludging tearfully out to the kitchen; Aunt Inez fluttering after her saying "Waste not, want not"; my sister running merrily upstairs, her enviable yellow ringlets bobbing, to play "Elevator" with the sliding doors in the hall or "Goodbye, Pants" with the laundry chute, so that she would inevitably get a finger smashed or a leg scraped and require the attention of the entire family before the evening was over; me stomping up to my bedroom with a volume of *Uncle Wiggily* held importantly under my arm; my father coming up slowly after me, in another attempt to tuck me in.

"What's wrong with my little Zaza?" he pleaded one night. "I haven't seen one single smile on your face since we got here!"

"I *told* you," I said. "I hate it here. I want to go home. I want to go to your *office*, like I used to, like I used to in New York, where we live. I never *get* to anymore!"

"Zaza, I *can't* take you to my office here," he said. "I'd like to, but I can't."

"Yes. I know, it's about the War Ever," I said cynically. As usual, I opened *Uncle Wiggily* to a picture that I recognized and pretended to read. Reading was a matter of moving your eyes back and forth and making understanding faces now and then.

"It's the war *effort*," my father said. "The war *effort*, like in *trying*. Because of the War Effort, I can't have guests in my office, not even little girls, because everything is secret. For example, Firestone makes tires for the Army."

I pictured giant tires dropping out of planes onto Hitler's head. "I already know about *tires*, Daddy," I said indignantly.

From out in the hall there came the shriek of my sister with

50

her thumb conveniently caught in the sliding door, and from downstairs the plaint of my mother, "Now nobody should interrupt themselves, but I am in considerable pain," and the sound of Jello snuffling and Aunt Inez, her birds twittering, singing "Look for the Silver Lining."

My father said, "Sometimes it is very important to the War Effort to help out at home." He stood up and tried to look very firm. He said, "You are my best and brightest, Zaza, and I definitely think you can help out at home a lot more than you have been doing. You could be a big help to me. Just a little smile now and then would help me."

"I know, Daddy," I said.

"Then why don't you help me?" he asked.

"I don't want to," I said. "I just want to go home."

"This is a very important job to me," said my father. "It is an *opportunity*. Do you know what an *opportunity* is?"

"Yes, Daddy," I said. I didn't, of course. "But I don't care." With his big words and funny problems, he sounded just like that hapless fellow Uncle Wiggily.

We glared at one another across the shiny picture of Uncle Wiggily where Nurse Jane Fuzzy Wuzzy is helping him across something called a stile. My father left, and I listened contentedly to my sister wailing as Mercurochrome was applied to her arm. A feeling of power was washing over me as I fell asleep, a feeling that I could somehow now move my family back East to the town where I belonged, with my jacks.

How I was to accomplish this began dimly to emerge a few days later, when Aunt Inez suddenly turned off a radio program featuring Great Organ Hymns. Aunt Inez said, "Why, this is so depressing! All these songs about death! I simply cannot abide thoughts of death, can you, Jello?"

Jello stopped crying and looked at Aunt Inez quizzically. "Yes, ma'am," said Jello. "I like hymns. I was raised with hymns. I like hymns very much."

So at this point I enlisted Jello and the piano as my allies. I had always circled the piano warily in New York, but my parents had hauled it to Ohio anyway, perhaps in the hope that I would somehow attack music with miraculous gusto in the smoky air of Akron.

This I did do now, conscripting Jello to help me learn to play "Nearer, My God, to Thee" and "The Old Wooden Cross." Her eyes brightened up considerably during our piano sessions.

Since Jello was about as inept as I was, the hymns took endless practice. Aunt Inez cowered in the kitchen, her birds drooping. "Why is the child always playing *hymns*?" she asked my father as soon as he came home from work. "I am so depressed. That child is always playing 'Nearer, My God, to Thee.' I can't abide that piece. It's about dying, and I am getting on in years, Lord knows!"

My father confronted me. "Why are you depressing your aunt with hymns about dying?" he asked.

"You *wanted* me to learn the piano," I said, "and I'm learning the piano and these are the only songs Jello and I know."

"Is that so, Jello?" said my father.

"Yes, sir," said Jello, clear-eyed.

"Well, there it is!" said Aunt Inez. "Catering to the whims of a child and a servant! Times have changed surely!"

"Now, Aunt," said my mother, jiggling her cast impatiently. "Now, Aunt, the child is showing some gift for music, and we all have every right to be happy about *that*." She fell sighing back into the chaise which my father had found for her at the same store where he had found a gas stove. An actual modern stove was hard to find during the War Ever.

The stove was supposed to be delivered on the same day that Aunt Inez and the birds were huffily scheduled to leave because of the hymns. My father was driving Auntie and the birds in their cages to the railroad depot, with Jello along just to help with Sweetie and Sillabub, after she was assured that she would not have to get out of the car until it came back to the house. "Now, Zaza," my father said to me warily, "I am leaving it to you to look out for the delivery man. Just look out the window for them, and direct them around to the back door. Don't have them come up the front steps, because they're too high. This is probably the last gas stove in Ohio, because of the War Ever."

"A stove, a real stove," exclaimed my mother, stomping about on her cast with unusual vigor and clapping her hands as I used to do back home after a superb jacks play. "A stove just like I had back East! Thank the Lord I won't have to feel like a pioneer lady anymore. I'm so tired of that ol' coal stove, aren't you, Jello?"

"Yes, Ma'am," said Jello as she happily toted the birds out the door. I settled down to my ally, the piano, and attempted to pick out the cheery "Country Gardens." My sister screamed from the bathroom that her hand was caught in the laundry chute, but my mother was too absorbed in her delight about the stove to hear her. Would my plan have a bonus? Would my sister be silenced forever in a mass of soiled linen? But her piping, Shirley Temple voice yelled very soon from an upstairs window. "Men are here with something!"

I dashed to the front door. "Bring it right up here," I hollered. "Bring it right up these front steps!"

I leaned out the window and watched with satisfied antici- pation as two men edged a gigantic stove up the first of several cement steps. By step five thay had, of course, lost it. The Last Gas Stove in Ohio crashed definitively down the stairs and landed with a crumpled bash in its side.

"Oh, my land!" said my mother, maneuvering out onto the stoop. "That stove'll never work now. Now you just take it back and get me a new one!"

"Can't do it, Lady," said one man sadly. "This was the very last stove."

"Oh, my Lord," said my mother. She was literally hopping mad when my father got home from the depot. "I am up to my neck!" she told him. "I am up to my *neck* in this part of the world!" She tugged Jello into the kitchen, where the two of them somehow managed to construct a meat loaf and baked potatoes for dinner.

"I cannot *abide* Ohio," said my mother later, vigorously slicing meat loaf. "It was bad enough I had to give up my New York frigidaire for an icebox, but now I am fated to that awful coal stove for the duration of the War. And," she added, "it may have escaped your attention, because I have been very silent about my pain, but I have been very unhappy here."

"Is that so?' said my father. "And how about my little Curly Top?" he said, turning to my odious little sister, with her bright smile and her millions of bandaids. "Do *you* like it here?"

"No," she said.

He never asked me. I don't think he said one word to me until long after we got back home to New York. I can't remember that he ever even told me about what my mother said was the marvelous *new* opportunity he had discovered back East. But I remember being sadly and smugly patient, as

Nurse Jane always was until Uncle Wiggily came round.

When Jello and I were sitting in the roomette on the eastbound train, I asked her "Is the War Ever over yet?" And she said, "I don't know, but Francis came home. He's down at Fort Bragg." She smiled as she hugged me.

Summer Writing Workshop
R.L. Tucker

Any could be, in age, my children.
They are innocent, knowing,
clumsy, graceful.

Shall I tint out gray? Wear designer jeans?
Disguise my age and pose as youth...
for now?

Not *be* young again, you understand
(not young and innocent, at least),
but masquerade.

Then would they judge my words alone,
blind to my decrepitude?

But I can not smooth facial lines,
excise experience;
I am the old man in Comp Two-Oh-Two.

❖

A Mystery

Jo McKim Chalmers

The little prick, in the center of a
button, placed on the generous breast
of an Oven Stuffer chicken, how long
had it thrust upwards, unnoticed as
Ms. Oso Lonely went about her
fateful hour?

As a bullet pierced her breast, she
wondered, for the wildest second,
if another's breast, in the dark-
ened cavern of the burnt-out-bulb
oven had, as yet, discharged
its signal?

The Oven Stuffer, by now a
deepened tan, was deemed
delicious. But, by whom?
Who found it so?
Who ate it up?
Who neatly stacked
its bones on table
set for one?

Mortal Merely

Jo McKim Chalmers

The gathering billlows peak, and crash.
The wind and the tide tug at me.
"I'm yours. I'm *yours*," I cry.
Only, I no longer wish
to be a mermaid:
to peer into the depths,
be caressed by tentacles of octopi,
hold drowned seamen
to my breast.

I am mortal, merely.
Safe and dry.
Until, one day,
a tidal wave
shall come
for me.

Dusk

Jo McKim Chalmers

Dusk has passed her hand along the beach:
gulls and pelicans have folded wings,
the surf laps listlessly,
the water's green has gone,
the yellow deck chairs, now bone white,
white clouds are grey.
The rioting sun
drops into the sea.
Big fish nose in closer to the shore
where smaller fish
seek safety through the night.

On the Threshold: 1954

Mary Leonard

I'm wearing my best, a blue cotton
Mother embroidered with cross stitches,
bordered with rickrack. It's June.
I dry my hair on the back porch
brushing my curls upside down
until they shine silver in the window,
my face a dark negative. Mother, always late,
powders her nose and plays with lipsticks.
Jubilee Cherry, Bermuda Coral? Not wanting
to miss the 10:25, I swirl on one Capezio toe
and announce, in the voice of my older sister,
"Coral for our movie star!" Mother picks
a piqué bolero, searches
for her keys and money hoarded
from her household allowance. I hold
the screen door, urging her on,
while watching Mr. Graham rise
from his patio chair and wave to me
with his high-held glass. Like Gatsby
I ache to cross to the other side
and lose who I am
in Mr. Graham's manicured maze
of evergreens and trellised roses.

The train's cool straw seats soothe my legs.
Women board at Bronxville and I envy
their smooth blonde flips, their leather purses.
To eavesdrop on their gossip I curl
like a rabbit while Mother makes lists:
sheets from the white sale at Altman's,
lingerie, something crisp and white for sister,

a dress from Bloomingdale's basement,
and my hair cut at Best & Co.
The conductor calls out the stations,
each syllable a song
                              Tuck a hoe   Tuck a hoe
The train sways, hypnotizes
and as we rise above city streets,
my eyes flicker, close, open to scenes
from old time movies: large women making beds
with billowy white sheets, thin men in undershirts
cooling on stoops.

In Altman's we march straight past the jewelry
to brass escalators. On Floor Two, Lingerie,
I enter a cave of lace and silk
and feel the sensuality of scenes
only glimpsed in Doris Day movies.
Mother and I examine the sale table, touching, opening,
searching for the gown we'll know when we see it.
We both circle my sister's wedding, I copying
brides from magazines, Mother adding to the trousseau
and her own dreams. We find two,
not too frilly, no décolletage, white and pristine.
Mother checks the fabric, the seams, showing me
at nine what the inside of a garment should look like,
and I see my mother, not much older than me,
sewing in dark rooms, lit only by sequins.

On a double-decker Fifth Avenue bus, I memorize
cabbage roses on wide picture hats
and pale lilacs burdening the sides of bowlers.
We pull the cord at St. Patrick's, visiting quickly,
only lighting one candle before exchanging incense
for Main Floor perfume. In Best's waiting room,
windowed to Rockefeller Center, I watch and want
to build my own skyscraper with blocks,
but feel too shy, too old, easier to snuggle
very close to Mother. Mr. Joseph cuts
my bangs two inches above my eyes, complains
about my curls, too many, too thick,
and I wish for straight hair he could turn

with his curling iron. I hold tight
to my pink and white balloon advertising Best & Co.,
ignoring whispers of "cute" from huddled salesgirls.

At Schrafft's the waitress wears all black, even her oxfords,
only her white apron and red curls distancing her
from Sister Pauline. We always order BLT's on toast,
tea for mother, a black-and-white soda for me.
I save the ice cream for Mother's stories, today, her wedding,
not the ruffled organdy dress, not the white gardenias,
but after, climbing the steps on West Forty Eighth,
Dad's brothers draped like mannequins around the kitchen
     table,
the windows, uncurtained, grey with the smoke of cigars,
and a silence she had never known. Mother's eyes glaze,
but I'm too young for the words she needs. I squirm
in my seat and whisper, "Let's leave."

At Bloomingdale's we find six print dresses, cheap,
in Mother's size. We laugh like school girls
when the dress is too tight or the ruffles bigger
than Mother's head. We find one, a pastel,
that makes Mother look like the movie star she should be,
but it's overpriced. She decides to send it C.O.D.,
saving on the tax, but doesn't feel right, I know,
so I don't insist on French crullers,
only orange Lifesavers for the train ride home,
the time we review the day, peeking at purchases,
wishing we didn't leave behind the pink peignoir.
Mother says, after the wedding, she'll shop just for me.
I dream of a camel hair coat, of penny loafers, of blonde hair.
My eyes open and close: a dark man resting
on a window sill lifts a can to his lip, my father
on our back porch hammers at a loose board,
reaches for his beer, and across our street, the Grahams
hold tightly to glasses of iced tea.
I step onto their patio, awnings flutter.
The conductor chants
                    Crest wood   Crest wood
I am cold. I hold my mother's hand.

61

--- ❖ ---

A Vietnam Protest: 1968

Mary Leonard

A Vietnam vet shoots
pool at the green table in the back
of Donnelly's, our place to brag
"after the revolution..." to feast
on hard-boiled eggs, beef jerky, any quick
fix so we can down draught beer
until Jimmy flicks the lights.
On the way to the john, three steps beyond
the pool table, I'm introduced.
I can't remember his name, only his hair—
long, blonde, tied back
with teeth, awful human trophies spitting
out his mane. At a keg party
by the falls we lean against each other
to smoke some weed and wander off
to crawl through poison ivy.
In the dark I don't see three shiny leaves,
the warning.

That night we separated from the others,
I fell over brambles, vines, while you
slashed through the thicket, never offering
your arm, only, "Get moving!"
You lunged. We kissed.
I pushed you away. You pushed me
aside to stick me with bits
about Nam, your buddies,
how I didn't understand.
Your words cut me off
from passion, sent me reeling
back to the fire, to my friends'

protests against the war. I abandoned you
in the thicket you could never leave
but you left your mark on me. Until they bled,
I scratched mounds of blisters, enemy ant hills,
my body's protests against poison leaves,
your warning of a new breed.

Ghosts

Tara McCarthy

Tomorrow night I will be gone from this house,
And it will be haunted.
The big window at the top of the stair will hold my reflection,
The ocean my eyes.
The bed will embrace the memory of my body,
And the shutters will knock insistently.

A little pile of yellow stones,
Two leaning, yearning spears of grass whipped by the
    May wind,
And a fox sparrow, darting below gulls,
With a treasure for nesting brought to the eaves:
You will miss my images of you.
Whoever else comes here will build other worlds.
No one else will see you as I do,
Or see you at all.

The Considerate Boyfriend

Tara McCarthy

My lover is a very nice lover.

He doesn't jump on me while I am reading.
He doesn't paw me at mealtime.
He doesn't ask me to take my clothes off after I have
    just finished dressing.

My lover is very considerate and subtle.
Like, when he sees a real hot movie star in a movie,
He just goes, "Wow, look at that" "Would I like to have
    a piece of that!"

Then after the movie, he says, "I hope you didn't take
    offense!" "I mean, she is a 10 definitely, but
    you are a ten and a half."

So eat the pizza slowly, because afterwards

You have to paw him and take your clothes off slowly, just to
show both of you that you are as wonderful
As he thinks the hot movie star is.

"Wow," he says, "I love an assertive, take-charge woman!"

So you lie there and sigh a lot as he jumps on his dream.
Meanwhile the movie star is probably reading the script for

Her next movie! which you will probably have to suffer
    through with this

Considerate Boyfriend.

Non-Poem

R.L. Tucker

An English sentence s
t
r
u
n
g

o
u
t

v
e
r
t
i
c
a
l
l
y

Is not a poem, but something much verse.

True Love

R.L. Tucker

Quite suddenly you throw the darts,
Sharp-tipped and venom-dipped;
You've never lost the knack
Of timing for complete surprise,
Your aim still accurate.
But, the number that sink deep
Has dropped, I'm sure, in recent years.
Perhaps desire has waned,
Or quarry's skin grown tough
In many vital places now?

A strange relationship has grown
Between your favorite game
And you who flush it out.
At times, transfixed, he smiles at you,
Your next dart poised to throw,
And you evince some slight
Reluctance then to hurl it home.
And why does he come back
Again to test your aim?
I know it sounds absurd, and yet,

Perhaps you feel affection for
The object of your hunt?
You two have been engaged
So long in this exotic sport,
You've come to know and need
What each of you can give.
So hone your pointed darts again,
Don't fear he'll not return.
He's tied to you and you to him
By bonds as strong as love.

Apple Tree

R.L. Tucker

A piece of our old apple tree
Came down last night in its own secret way.
It must have been while I was gone in sleep
That it gave in to apples' weight
And rotting wood, and groaned once quietly,
Then toppled in a rush to earth.

In early light I saw the world had changed
But could not tell just what it was
That made my window landscape ominous.
I felt some intimation of mortality
Chill my heart before the broken tree
Became apparent to my eye and brain.

My instant thought concerned the cost
Of clearing death away. No sooner thought
Than I was mortified, as though
Some old friend's funeral had interfered
With playing golf one day. Ashamed,
I shambled out to face the corpse.

Reality exposed my morbid images
As solely from within; the apple tree
Still lived, if badly needing paring down.
I moved from fine clichés to toothéd saws
And pruning tools—sure cures for maudlin sentiment—
And sweated out my foolish gloom in woodsman's toil.

But not without reward:
Sweet firewood, some twenty lines of verse,
And aching joints of truth.

Whatever You Do

Adele LeBlanc

Velma Mansfield sat cross-legged on the end of the big brass bed that she had shared for six years with Bertram Mansfield. To his friends in the world of poetry he was known as Bart Mansfield, but to Velma he would always be Bertram. It was a Sunday evening, and as usual the Mansfields were engaged in their separate activities. Bart had thrown on his trench coat and carefully wrapped his long neck in the white silk scarf that Velma had given him for Christmas and made his way to the Calliope Coffeehouse where he was scheduled to read his new ode entitled "Credulity." Velma had descended eleven floors to the basement Laundromat where she had done the week's wash and the Sunday *Times* Crossword...the first in a new detergent for which she had a coupon and the second in pencil with a smudgy eraser.

Now she sat on the bed and bent low to the work of mismatching Bertram's socks. Behind her through the partly opened window, she could hear raindrops beginning to hit the grating of the fire escape. It was the end of a warmish January week and Bertram, who always kept up on the latest weather developments, had informed her before he went out that it would turn sharply colder tonight and that there was a fifty percent chance of snow by morning.

"Oh to be somewhere where I could hear rain hit a roof again," Velma said as she paired the last two socks, a red argyle and a dingy gray jogging sock. She had been mismatching his socks for approximately nine months, about as long as it would have taken to have a baby, and Bertram had never seemed to notice. He never seemed to notice the absence of a baby either.

"I *did* love him," she said in a precise, loud voice, justifying the last six years of her life to her grandmother's mantel clock, which clucked back at her. Velma recognized this new ten-

69

dency to speak her thoughts out loud as a definite problem.

But she flopped back onto the bed and let herself remember taking a night flight to New York from Birmingham to marry Bertram Mansfield, poet.

Manhattan was their honeymoon. They walked the streets of the city and Velma found herself surprised by the stench of the summer heat, disturbed by the unrelenting noise of sirens, pneumatic drills and brakes, and the clamor of people speaking in foreign tongue.

Bertram described the magic feeling that he had for this city to her, but she felt only its reality when passing pedestrians stepped on her feet. There were so many of them, and try as she might, she could not get out of their way in time. She dreaded most those wearing the thick cowboy boots so much in fashion.

Bertram worked for the Merrie Greeting Card Company. Of course for them he produced light verse. As he told Jane Van Dylan-Duke and Morris Stutz at the coffee house, "It's only doggerel."

He reserved his serious work for the evenings, sometimes working late into the night, even on their honeymoon. Once during those first two weeks, Velma had gotten up in the middle of the night to go to the bathroom. Bertram had left the light on over his desk, and there was a piece of paper in his typewriter.

It was like a piece of forbidden fruit, because he had never let her read his work, not in all the months of their long-distance courtship. "You should be writing yourself, creating," he would say to her. "Don't depend on others for creativity. Create something of your own."

Velma approached the desk quietly. She could hear Bertram's steady snores from the brass bed. She sat tentatively on the edge of his chair, ready to let her eyes take in her husband's words, ready to let her mind, as well as her body, merge with that of Bertram Mansfield or perhaps even with that of Bart Mansfield. She shivered in excitement, and this is what she read:

> As down life's path we forward trod,
> Finding ways both narrow and broad,
> My heart will hark back to the day
> When your eyes urged me to say

There the poet had broken off. Velma rubbed her eyes and read the poem again...slowly. Then she got to her feet. "This is serious?" she queried in her new mock Brooklyn accent. "This *is* serious," she replied in her Southern drawl. There were seven wadded balls of paper on the table. Velma did not unfold any of them. Instead she went into the bathroom. As she flushed the toilet she glanced at the unfinished *Times* Crossword that she had left on the side of the bathtub. It was then that she began to cry. She continued to cry in the kitchen while she made a pot of coffee and even when she began to read Proust. She was reading the volume entitled *The Captive* and she was fascinated and after a time she stopped crying.

That had been six years ago. Tonight she folded her memory of reading Bertram's poetry and put it away with his clean underwear. Once again her life seemed spun dry.

It was the following week that Samuel M. Hobbs had come to be Velma's new boss at the Midtown Auto Parts Company. Mr. Hobbs showed up for work at Midtown dressed in a three-piece suit. Velma figured he was out to make a good impression on Abe Koppel, the president of the small firm. Abe himself was strictly a shirtsleeves executive. In fact when the air conditioning had faltered the previous August, he had stripped down to his undershirt. At the end of the first week at work, Mr. Hobbs still had not removed his jacket, but he had unbuttoned it to display an impressive gold chain stretched across the front of his vest.

"They say old man Koppel hired him to bring some class to the place," Honey Evers whispered to Velma on their coffee break. "I think he's doing it, too, bringing class I mean. I think he's adorable." Honey picked at her nail polish. It was a very bright shade of pink that Velma remembered hearing her give some kind of seashell, seashore name to.

"Don't you think he's adorable?" Honey was giggling, actually giggling. She was too old to be giggling. It didn't become her.

"Hello, Velma, are you there?" Honey was poking her in the ribs.

"No, I don't think he's adorable," she answered, deciding then and there.

"You wouldn't, but maybe it will impress you to hear that they say he was Phi Beta Kappa at Yale. They say that he wears

71

a Phi Beta Kappa key on that chain around his cute middle. That's the kind of thing that would probably impress you. We'll divide him up. You can have the brains. I'll take the body. You should have seen the look on his face when I said to him in my most seductive voice, 'Just call me Honey.' Most of the time when I've seen that look on a man's face, it's been in the sanctity of my own boudoir. I mean the man reeks of sex."

Honey spent the rest of the coffee break fantasizing about a possible date with Mr. Hobbs. Honey was somewhere over thirty-five and unmarried.

Velma had her first scheduled conference with Mr. Hobbs that afternoon, and as he carefully closed the door of his office to emphasize the privacy of their talk, Velma sniffed the air for the smell of sex. She was not sure she remembered what it smelled like.

"Well, Velma, I'm glad we're finding time for a little talk." He flashed her a brilliant smile.

Right on cue, Velma thought to herself.

"And I want us to be on a first name basis here," he continued. "I want to have a very open management style. I want to have a real open door policy."

Velma glanced toward the closed door.

"I want you to feel that you can come to me with anything and get a listen from me."

"Is this Yale Business School lingo?" Velma literally bit her tongue as she said it, but she said it. She couldn't help herself.

He had been playing with a pen while they talked. The pen fell to the desktop and there was only the slightest of pauses before he leaned so far back in his executive chair that Velma thought he must surely topple over backward. His laughter, when it came, seemed as broad as the Hudson and as tall as the Twin Towers. His blue eyes twinkled at her, pulling a smile to her lips in spite of herself. She took a deep breath and let the sweet smell of sex overwhelm her.

At home the next Sunday night Velma attacked the week's laundry in a most desultory manner. The first time she took the elevator to the basement, she forgot her supply of quarters. Then she forgot to put in the fabric softener. All the while she stared at the crossword puzzle, unable to get beyond the upper left-hand corner. Finally she broke her pencil point and opened Proust in desperation only to find that she had lost her place and that suddenly every page looked the same.

All the socks looked the same too when she sat on the bed trying to mix her matches. She wanted to cry but couldn't find any good reason for doing so.

Later when Bertram turned his key in the lock and made his usual grand gesture of removing his topcoat, she could not wait to fling herself into his arms. It seemed to surprise him greatly and he avoided her kiss by muttering something about a sore throat and germs. In bed she could not get warm. Then she was finally able to cry because the sound of Bertram's typing was keeping her awake.

At work that week, Sam Hobbs continued scheduling his little management chats with the rest of the staff. He had a particularly long chat with Liza from the typing pool. It lasted through the lunch hour and Mr. Hobbs sent out for pastrami sandwiches and coleslaw. It was said that Liza was going to be given new responsibilities.

"She may even become his private secretary," Honey told Velma confidentially. "Do you think they're having an affair?"

"An affair? How romantic!" Velma said. "Do you mean do I think he's screwing her? Well, the answer to that is *yes*. I don't think people have affairs any more."

"On the soaps they do," Honey said.

"How would you know? You're never home to watch them."

"I have had several affairs," Honey took the last bite of her morning's Danish. "I had one last year."

Velma hoped this was true.

The other women in the office drew nearer to Liza suddenly. They went to the water fountain when she did, sharpened their pencils at the same time, crowded onto the elevator with her at five, hoping that she would speak. Hoping that she would reveal to them all the delicious mysteries of Samuel M. Hobbs. Was he married? Had he ever been? Was there hair on his chest? Did he take her to nice restaurants on his expense account and what did they eat? What did he drink? What did he talk about in bed? They had been to bed, hadn't they? Even Velma wondered these things, and she wondered why she wondered.

Liza, for her part, said not a word about Sam Hobbs, not even when Mr. Hobbs began to consider Evelyn Ferguson for the Executive Secretary position. One Monday morning Liza was seen with the want ad section open on her desk. By that Friday she was gone to a much higher-paying job, or so they said. On that same Friday Mr. Hobbs and Evelyn had peanut butter sandwiches for their working lunch and by Monday morning Evelyn was out of the running and Trisha was under serious consideration.

Unlike Liza, Evelyn talked. She said that he had a wife and kid in Westchester, that he had no hair on his chest, was a cheapskate, and was lousy in bed.

"Sour grapes," Honey muttered.

Velma had listened to all of this very carefully. She was most apprehensive when she found the note on her desk asking her to schedule a meeting with him at ten the next morning.

At nine thirty she dialed Bertram at the Merrie Greeting Card Company. He was coughing when he answered and she couldn't think of what to say, so she asked him to pick up milk on the way home.

"For Pete's sake, there's a half gallon in the fridge. What are you planning on making?" He blew his nose loudly. "I'm feeling awful," he said.

"So am I," she said as she hung up.

She went to the ladies' room and combed her hair. She started to put on fresh lipstick and then didn't. "I must be crazy," she said out loud.

Behind the closed door of his office, Sam Hobbs motioned her to be seated on the couch. He stood at the desk shifting piles of papers. "Thank you so much for coming, Mrs. Mansfield." He gave her a look that was serious, solemn, and sincere. All that, and not a hint of a smile.

"Velma," she said.

"Oh, yes, Velma. Well, Velma, I am throwing myself on your mercy." He came to sit in the large overstuffed chair to her left. "Throwing myself on your mercy," he repeated, leaning slightly toward her. He cleared his throat. "You must have noticed that I have been conducting a whole series of interviews with various staff members." His voice was hesitant, almost trembly. "And, er, I have failed to find the person with the suitable qualifications to become my Executive Secretary." His tone capitalized every letter of the title.

My God, Velma thought, I don't want to be this man's secretary. I don't want to be anyone's secretary. She shifted on the couch and a pillow fell to the floor.

"Mind you," he raised a hand in protest, "I'm not suggesting for one minute that I would consider a person of your stature for a secretarial position. In fact, Velma, I have wondered why a person with your obvious intellectual capabilities is wasting time working in a company like this." He fingered the gold chain at his waist.

"What about you? What exactly are you doing here?" she asked.

"You're wonderful, Velma. That's a terrific no-shit answer to what must seem like some very ingratiating remarks from me. But they're heartfelt you know, and as for me, I don't intend to spend my entire career at Midtown, but it's a place where I can try to put in practice what they said they had taught me when they gave me that certificate at Yale. Sort of hone my skills, you know."

"I just never expected to see a Phi Beta Kappa key at Midtown," she smiled at him.

He seemed to be almost counting the links on the chain as his smile came back to her. "So they talk about that at coffee break, do they?"

He didn't wait for her reply. "What I need from you, Velma, is help in locating the right person. With your intelligence and what I sense is your fantastic intuition, I know you can be an immense help to me in the screening process. It may well be that there is no one here at Midtown to fit the bill and in that case, I'd like to turn the whole business of running ads and contacting agencies over to you. You could pass along only the candidates you thought were right for me. Would you consider doing that? It would be such a help. If you want to think it over, just take your time. Let me know what you think in the next few days."

"I don't need to think it over," she said. "I'll do it, but you'll have to tell me exactly what you are looking for. And, Sam, are you always so serious?" It all came out in a rush and she didn't know why she had said any of it.

He laughed with her then, for she *was* laughing. "Let's have a non-serious drink after work and I'll go over what I consider to be the most important qualifications."

At McMichael's Bar she found that he drank Bombay gin and smoked a pipe, but she didn't find out anything about the job qualifications. He gestured a lot with the pipe, lit it innumerable times, and talked about a certain indefinable quality. "I'd like to think," he said, "that if nothing else comes of this, we will have at least gotten to know each other better. I'm sure that I could start by asking those pedestrian questions about where you live, where you worked before Midtown, whether you have kids, what your husband does. But then you in turn would ask those same questions of me, and I don't choose to talk about my wife and daughter because then I would become serious again, and we don't want that to happen. What I truly want to know is what you do. I mean, what keeps you from going crazy reporting to that dumb company of ours each Monday morning? You must have something wonderfully fulfilling in your life to be able to put up with the boredom of Midtown."

She wasn't sure he wanted an answer. She pushed her chair back from the table, assessing the situation. She was sitting at a bare wooden table in a dark bar in the middle of Manhattan on a late Friday afternoon in February. Outside it might be snowing. The streets might be starting to collect the dirty slush that came with any snowfall in the city. Inside the smells of smoke, beer, and fried food hung in the air and customers' voices got suddenly louder. They were talking in their weekend voices now, strong and clear.

"What are you thinking?" he leaned halfway across the table to make sure she heard.

She was thinking that at age thirty-four she was sitting in this bar across this table from a good-looking man. You might almost say handsome man. She *would* say handsome man and that the man who just might be a few years younger than herself just might find her attractive and that, in any case, he had asked her a question requiring a thoughtful answer. No one had done that in years. She thought all these things, but she didn't say any of them. Instead she said something that she never would have thought she would say.

"I write."

"You what?"

She had spoken very softly.

"You asked what I do, well, I write." It was only a partial lie. She wrote elaborate scenarios, exotic fables, lyrical poems, but only in her head. Still she wrote them.

"Why, I think that's wonderful! When I was in college I had

76

a very Hemingwayesque story published in the literary quarterly and I gave real thought to becoming a writer myself. Then I began to understand that about half of the sophomores in the U.S. had published Hemingwayesque stories that year and I gave it all up."

He looked at her with calm, kind eyes. She felt that he was looking at a Velma that no one else saw, one that she herself had caught a glimpse of once in a mirror on the night of her senior prom and had always hoped to see again. She felt as young as a cheerleader. She had never been a cheerleader. She was smiling to herself and at him and she couldn't stop herself.

"You know, it's probably been a long time since McMichael's has seen someone as radiant as you are right now," he said.

She could not tolerate his compliment. "I'm writing a novel," she said hurriedly.

The novel. That was an absolute lie, no halfway measures about that. She felt the guilt take over. "I should be home working on it right now. I really have got to go."

"That does it," he said. "You force me to ask where you live."

"Brooklyn. You know, the borough where cabbies don't go."

He tapped the ashes from the bowl of his pipe into the ashtray. Then he reached across the table and touched the back of her hand lightly. "You are just what I need right now," he said slowly. "I am in great need of someone to talk to, someone who sees right through the bullshit of banalities. Please say we can do this again."

She already had her coat half on. She didn't want him to help her with it.

"We can," she said, "of course we can."

She spent her weekend thinking. Thinking of her six years of marriage, of her childhood in Alabama, of bleaching her hair, of her first boyfriend, a boy named Chip. Mostly she was thinking of her novel. It almost became real. She thought it might be about her ancestors' pioneer days in the forests of western Alabama.

It didn't seem like Sunday night, even when she heard Bertram in the bathroom brushing his teeth and gargling, getting ready to head out for the Calliope. She realized that she had no plans, no intention of doing the laundry. It's time I bought new underwear, she decided. The question of Bertram's socks never entered her mind. The usual Sunday night dread, the threat of the impending work week was not with her and she was just beginning to sense that. She didn't understand its absence, but she was beginning to enjoy herself.

She was lying in the exact middle of the brass bed staring at a soiled spot on the ceiling to the left of the light fixture when Bertram came to tell her goodbye.

"Don't you feel well?" he asked. "Maybe you've got a touch of that flu that's going around. Jane's been fighting it off for over a week now."

"What would you say if I told you I was thinking about writing a novel?" she asked.

"Great! I've been telling you for years to get your creative juices flowing. Jane has always said that you look like a very poetical person to her. She has always said that she wouldn't be surprised to have you turn up at the Calliope some night with something of your own to read. I think you should just go right ahead. Tell me more about it later, okay? I'm running late."

She lay there after he left, wondering if he was screwing Jane Van Dylan-Duke. It had never occurred to her to wonder that before. She laughed out loud thinking that he would never bed a woman who was fighting off the flu. The germs!

Velma and Sam arrived at the entrance to their office building on 46th Street at precisely the same time the next morning. "Wow, you look great this morning! What did you do to your hair?" he asked.

How could he know that she had thought about bleaching it? She hadn't bleached it. She had only thought about bleaching it. Maybe she had bleached it and was suffering a sudden amnesia. She decided to take a good look in the ladies' room mirror as soon as they reached their floor.

"I've got a couple of other secretarial candidates to see from the staff today," he went on, "but it's obvious to me that I'm probably going to want to see others, so if you have time this morning, I'd like you to move right ahead with contacting the agencies. Get some more bodies in here pronto."

His use of the word "bodies" made her wince and she thought he noticed.

"By the way," he said, "I thought about you over the weekend. I thought about you a lot. I want you to know that I appreciate all you're doing to help out, but I also want you to know that I appreciate you as a person."

When she hurried into the ladies' room for a look at herself, her hair did look different, in fact, her whole face looked like it had been made up for some kind of color photograph. She discovered that she was blushing.

"Hey, Velma, have you lost weight or what?" Honey was staring at the technicolor reflection along with her.

"Not that I know of...but I don't remember pigging out like I usually do over a weekend...just had no appetite."

"Well, it becomes you. I hear Casanova has a meeting lined up today with Faye and one tomorrow with Lin-Su. Just what he needs, huh? A Chinese secretary. It's even said that some saw you leaving the building with him Friday night, so I want you to feel free to give me all the glorious details. A girl's got to confide in someone. That's what I always say. If he ever treated me to an afternoon on his couch, I would tell you all about it. You are the only true friend that I have in this office, and I thought the feeling was mutual, so what do you have to say for yourself?"

"Strictly business, Honey. That's all it was. He asked me to help with interviewing his candidates and I agreed. He's really a nice man, Honey, and I think we may be accusing him falsely of fooling around with the women in the office. He *is* married, you know, and has a daughter."

"That makes a real difference," Honey sneered, "and it probably explains why Trisha went into his office one day last week with that nice beige blouse buttoned clear up to her neck and came out with it half unbuttoned, and the half that was buttoned, buttoned crooked at that. They were no doubt just having a long, intimate chat about his wonderful family."

That week as the personal agencies began to generate Sam's required bodies, Velma eyed carefully the clothing of each woman she sent in to see him. She didn't think she spotted a single dishevelled blouse or skirt askew, but she couldn't be sure.

Twice they went to McMichael's to hash over the candidates he had seen. "I've noticed one thing," he said as he took the first sip of his gin. "I almost hate to mention it to you, but it's a quirk I have." He stopped, considering the tobacco in his pouch. "No, I don't think I should mention it."

"You can't do that, Sam. If there's something wrong with the women I've been sending in to see you, you must tell me.

Otherwise, we're never going to find the right one."

He laughed. "You're right as usual and after all, it's something as simple as the size of their bosoms."

"What?" she couldn't believe that she had heard him correctly, but it was quiet in McMichael's on a Wednesday afternoon.

"Bosoms," he repeated, "well, hell, tits. They all have these big tits, and I don't like women with big tits; can't stand them. I like a woman who's shaped more like you, womanly and yet not ostentatious, if you know what I mean."

The burden of his blunt words fell heavily on her and then eased off into the kind of compliment that she had been waiting most of her life to hear.

"Now, don't start giving me some big women's lib lecture about how I'm not supposed to notice a woman's body. When I look at a woman I view her as a complete entity. I either buy the whole package or not at all. Oh, why can't you be my secretary...no, I don't mean that. You'll just have to be around to hold my hand during the process," he reached across and took Velma's hand in his, "and afterwards. You'll have to keep on holding it. I'm going to need you."

From that moment, Velma began to need him very badly.

The course that Velma and Sam followed from there to the Starbrite Motel on Routes 1 and 9 in New Jersey was tantalizing, timorous, and torturously slow. They had both come to recognize the need to get away somewhere alone together. Somewhere out of the midtown area, somewhere quiet where they could really talk and get to know each other. It had only been two weeks since he had first taken her hand in his, but it seemed like forever to Velma. One day at lunch they found themselves alone in one of the elevators, and without speaking a word, they had drawn together in a long kiss that kept Velma's blood churning all afternoon.

She had simply stopped seeing Bertram at home, much less hearing him. He must have been there, but for her, he was nonexistent. The laundry overflowed its basket and spilled out onto the bedroom floor. Her grandmother's mantel clock fell silent and the ice build-up in the freezer reached alarming proportions. Once she thought she heard Bertram inquiring about her health and she mumbled something back about feeling fine, about being preoccupied with her writing.

She was indeed writing. In her mind, she was writing the novel of her new life with Sam. They would live somewhere in the country, somewhere upstate in the mountains. They would live in a house where she would hear the rain on the roof and they would have a garden and farm animals and live off the land. They would sit by the fire on a winter's evening. They would not watch television. They would not have television. Instead he would read to her in his deep, melodious voice from Shakespeare's sonnets while the smoke of his pipe filled the air. And then they would go to bed and make love until the sun sparkled through the frosted pane in early morning. They would have children, of course, two girls and two boys, and all would look beautifully like Sam. This was a novel that bore much rewriting and with each revision, new details were etched in for her delight.

The realism of planning the trip to the Starbrite in New Jersey intruded itself upon her work on the novel. It upset her. She didn't want to use the word "sordid," but it came close to being the right word. Still on the day of the journey, she remembered to wear the new lace panties and bra that had cost her far too much at Saks.

At the Park and Lock lot, Sam had misplaced his stub and had to pay the full day's rate. "Not to worry," he told her. "I'll expense account it."

She wondered if he were expense accounting the entire trip.

When he turned the key in the ignition, the car's tape deck came on at full volume playing a Beach Boys recording. He didn't turn it down even when they got stuck in the tedious pace of crosstown traffic. The Lincoln Tunnel was one long traffic jam filled with sickening exhaust fumes. The Beach Boys were singing "Good Vibrations" and Sam, singing right along with them, beat out the rhythm on the top of his dash. Velma thought she might be sick. She tried to think about her novel.

On the New Jersey side of the river, she shut her eyes against a landscape cluttered with fast-food stands, half-abandoned factories, and lots full of rusting used cars. She didn't open them again until Sam pulled into a parking spot at the Starbrite. He insisted that she accompany him into the Office. Like the name said, the lobby was a bright place, full of pink neon lights in the shape of stars. And there for all to see were Velma and Sam registering at a motel in the middle of an afternoon.

"How many nights, sir?" the clerk asked.

"Oh, just the one night," Sam answered.

A lie, Velma thought. We can't spend the night. He has to go home to his family and I have to...she couldn't complete the thought.

She watched as Sam signed the register. He was signing his own name. He was signing Mr. and Mrs. Sam M. Hobbs. She didn't know what she had expected him to write, but somehow she hadn't expected him to spell out his full, real name. The pink stars beamed down on the fact of their afternoon's dalliance, but she must not think of it in that way.

The room was small, dark, and musty. It held one straight-back chair, one dresser with a mirror atop that tilted toward the one double bed. They both sat down heavily on the side of the bed.

She tried to think of something to do or say. Finally she said, "I don't even know your middle name."

His laughter warmed the room. "I wouldn't tell it to just anybody. Most of my life it's been my own dark secret, shared by about three people other than my mother who must have been crazy to give it to me. But you I'll tell. It's Makepeace."

"Makepeace?"

"Yes, as in Thackeray. You know William Makepeace Thackeray." He laughed again and started to help her out of her coat. "Very literary, don't you think? Just say to yourself that you're going to bed with a very literary man."

"Am I going to bed with you?"

"Of course."

He never stopped talking to her. During foreplay, during the act itself and afterward, his voice droned on. Velma had never heard anything like it. The few other men she had known under these circumstances had restricted their remarks to an occasional endearment, a dirty word or two, or in the case of some, to moans and groans. But his words encircled their lovemaking and she found herself enjoying the words almost more than the sex. What Evelyn had said, had some truth to it.

"We can't stay. You know that don't you?" he asked tentatively, tenderly. She nodded. "I'm going to grab a quick shower and we'd best be on our way."

She heard him start to sing "Good Vibrations" again as the shower pulsed on. Barefoot, she stepped over to the dresser intending to tilt the mirror so that she could search the bare skin of her body for the impression he must have made. She was sure she would be able to see something, but as she looked down at his gold chain lying on the dresser top, she forgot about the mirror. Attached to the end of the chain was a Masonic emblem. There was no mistaking it. Her grandfather had been a Mason. She had seen too many of them.

She was holding it in her hand when he came from the bathroom. "What happened to your Phi Beta Kappa key?" she asked.

"I never said I had a Phi Beta Kappa key," he grinned. "*You* said I had a Phi Beta Kappa key."

"Are you a Mason?"

"Hell, no. That's just something I picked up in a pawn shop one time down in Atlantic City. Sort of a joke."

"My grandfather was a Mason and he didn't think it was a joke."

"Now, Velma, don't go getting angry on me. We're both going to have to come down off the high of this sex thing. We're both going to have to face up to the rest of the world out there and especially the world at Midtown tomorrow morning, and we can't do that if we let anger get in our way. Besides, I'm looking at you right now, and I'm thinking you look like one of those Bennington College girls that I used to dream about when I was younger, the real artistic type with lots to offer in the brains department and a body that would make you know that you didn't care about the brains at all. Please say that we can do this again."

She thought she had heard him say something like that before, but she nodded anyway.

Honey pulled her into the coffee room the next morning. "You are going to tell me that you and Sam Hobbs spent the afternoon going around to personnel agencies yesterday, and I'll say I believe you if you will give me just one little juicy detail."

"It's a deal," Velma said. She decided it would not be too much of a betrayal to reveal his middle name. She would swear Honey to secrecy. She had had this great need lately to talk to someone about her relationship with Sam and this was about as close as she dared come to doing that. "His middle name is Makepeace."

"What?" Honey shrieked.

"I said his middle name...the M., it stands for Makepeace as in William Makepeace Thackeray. The writer," she added as she saw the puzzled look on Honey's face.

"My God, I thought that's what you said. What an appropriate name! He's certainly made every piece in this office."

Velma left the room, slamming the door behind her.

Weeks passed, leaving a string of motels and secretarial candidates in their wake. Velma had begun to think of her relationship with Sam as an affair, no matter that she had told Honey there was no such thing anymore.

One morning at home, Bertram asked her to call him in sick to Merrie. He had to make this request three times before she finally heard him, but then in a moment of contrition, she decided to go to work late herself so that she could make him a breakfast tray. When she opened the refrigerator, she was shocked to find only a bottle of seltzer and a dried-up orange. Bertram must have been eating out. She couldn't remember what she had been eating.

She opened a can of chicken noodle soup and took it to him. Another shock. He had grown a beard and it had some gray in it. It had the effect of making him look less poetic and more masculine. She thought fleetingly of Jane Van Dylan-Duke. Before she could remark on the beard, the phone rang and she couldn't believe it when she heard Sam's voice.

"Don't panic," he said. "It's perfectly natural for your boss to call. After all, you're an hour late and I need to know if you're coming in. I hope you are, Velma, because I need to talk to you. Something really special has come up and I'm hoping you can meet me at the Palm Court...you know, the Plaza at noon. We can talk and afterward, we can go upstairs. It'll be a special time for us. The Plaza's a special place."

"I'm sorry I didn't call in, Mr. Hobbs, but my husband's ill. I do plan on coming in, and yes, I can be there for that special meeting at lunchtime." She chose her words carefully and hung up before Sam could say more. "My boss," she told Bertram, "wanting to know if I could be there by lunchtime for a special meeting. I think I like your beard," she said as she left.

On the subway trip into Manhattan, she thought more about Bertram than she had in weeks. It wasn't until she walked into the Plaza that it occurred to her to wonder what this meeting was all about.

Sam was seated at a small table under a large palm, waiting for her. There was a pot of tea, a cup, and a room key on the table. "You won't have to watch me sign any register today," he said. "Old college chum of mine has taken over the job of afternoon desk manager and this one's on the house. Let's go straight up and enjoy the room. We can always send for room service, but this is so special I don't think I could eat a bite if I tried."

Sex at the Plaza was not vastly different from sex at the Starbrite. Oh yes, the room was wonderful...one of those with a view of Central Park, but Sam was Sam. He papered the walls of that room with his phrases just as he had done at the Starbrite. For the first time Velma thought that if he were a radio, she would turn him off.

"What's come up that's so special?" she kept asking.

"Later...I'll tell you all about it later. Maybe I won't tell you about it at all," he teased. "Sometimes I think you take notes when we're together like this. Sometimes I think you're planning to put all of it into your novel. You wouldn't do that, would you, Velma?"

It was something she had never thought of doing. She had been busy writing their future.

"Got to have my nice, hot shower now," he rose from the bed.

She turned to him suddenly. "Why do you always do that? Why do you always have to have a shower afterward? Do you think of me as being dirty? Do you feel you have to wash your contact with me down the shower drain?" She was beginning to sound hysterical.

"Don't be silly, Velma. It has nothing to do with you. It's just that the hot water in my bathroom at home has been on the fritz for the last couple of years. My wife yells, but I tell her I'm not calling in the plumber for a problem that I can handle perfectly well myself. See, I don't want to tackle that project until I have the time to put in a totally new bathroom, sunken tub, and everything. So, whenever I find myself in a hotel room, I grab a hot shower while I can...like I'm going to right now. Then when I'm all done, I'll tell you my big secret."

With the noise of the running water in her ears, Velma wondered first if his wife had managed to go to any hotel rooms in the last two years. Then she remembered last spring when she got so angry at Bertram for waiting a week to call their building super about the leaky kitchen faucet.

She glanced at herself in the full-length mirror on the facing wall and thought that she looked more like Velma than she did a cheerleader today.

He was quickly out of the shower with one of the Plaza's thick towels wrapped around his waist. "I did myself quite a favor last evening," he said. "I put my signature to quite a contract. A honey of a deal."

"You're talking like a Yalie," she said.

"As well I should be. I'm going to work for one of the big eight accounting firms in one of their key departments in a really high-level spot. High pay, too, I might add."

"Which firm?" she asked.

"Oh, I'm not at liberty to disclose that yet. Not even to you. But I start a week from Monday and as soon as I get set up in my new office, I'll give you a ring and we'll have lunch. I guess what I'm trying to say, Velma, is that I don't want anything to be different where you and I are concerned just because I'm moving to a new job. You know that, don't you? But I think it's inevitable that we won't get to see as much of each other. I'm probably going to have to spend a lot of my time in the downtown office and we both know about transportation difficulties in Manhattan. We won't lose this special friendship that we have though. You have gotten me through a really rough time in my life and I want you to know that I'll always be grateful. Who knows, I might just move ahead with getting a divorce once I get settled in the new job. New job...new life. Sounds great, doesn't it?" He smiled at himself in the mirror, showing all his teeth, turning slightly from side to side, taking stock of himself.

"One thing I will ask of you, Velma. Whatever you do, please don't write about us. Somehow when you try to write about something like we've had, it comes out sordid instead of beautiful the way we know it was."

How strange that he had chosen that word "sordid"...the very word that had hovered in Velma's mind as they planned their first trip to the Starbrite.

"But you can't leave yet," she said. She was crying and laughing and getting dressed all at the same time. "We haven't found your secretary yet."

"Poor baby," he said, and touched the back of his hand to her cheek, stopping a tear.

They didn't kiss good-bye. It would have been a gesture too inappropriate and final.

If Velma had been truly honest with herself, she would have admitted that she was glad to get home that day. She had stopped at the deli and picked up enough food to give the refrigerator a lived-in look.

Bertram refused to let her bring him a dinner tray. He put on his paisley robe and insisted on joining her at the dinner table. When she brought the food from the kitchen, she saw that he had lit candles. At bedtime he announced that he was going to kiss her goodnight, germs or no germs. I did love him, Velma reminded herself as she turned into Bertram's arms and then was not sure who she meant.

On Sunday night, Bertram felt well enough to go to the Calliope. He had written two new haiku. He hadn't let Velma see either one, but said that if the group at the Calloipe thought they were any good, he would read them to her. He might even dedicate them to her.

The minute he was out the door, Velma dragged the stepladder over to her closet. Standing on a top rung, she reached far back on the highest shelf until she found her old Smith Corona portable. She set it up on the bedroom table near the overflowing laundry basket, and with paper borrowed from Bertram's desk, she began to write.

Meeting Karen

Leslie Gerber

Whenever Harold thought about doing it, he imagined television reporters talking to people. Mrs. Simpson, for example. Her shriveled-up, brown pruneface, fishmouth popping open and closed: "He always had a moment to spend when he dropped by with the mail. Always a smile, something about the weather. Who would ever have thought..." Or the superintendent, Kowalski, bald and shiny as his water pipes: "Always paid his rent on time, never made any trouble with garbage or noise. Didn't seem like the most social fella, but he was always friendly. I would never have..."

Or even, God forbid, his mother. If she had any warning at all that something was coming, she'd be wearing that stupid red wig that didn't look like any hair God ever made to grow on a person, and she would probably have knocked back a quick one or two. "Harold was always such a *polite* child. Never made any trouble in school, respected his parents, did his chores just right. From the time he was five, I never even had to make his bed for him. *Never* any crayons on the floor, stains on the sheets. Why, I can't *believe* that..."

He had many other pictures like that in his head: the headline on the *Daily News*, the sound of the reporter's voice on News 88, the look on the cop's face, the judge. But they were never clear enough to suit him, nothing you could tack up on the wall. And those were just the peripheral items. The events themselves, the horror, his feeling of power, crossing the line for good, those important things were still so vague it disturbed him. I don't know if I can do this, he thought sometimes. I read about people doing things like this and it seems right for me, but how do I know I can actually do it. He would console himself by saying, When it happens, it will be clear enough. *Then* it will be real. But it bothered him not knowing how many times he could do it, if he would ever succeed with it at all.

But when it got too confusing, too far away for him to touch, he could always bring it back clearer by thinking about the whore. The red wig, just like his mother's, the long, bare legs, the awful color of the walls, the sheets, her crooked smile, the way her fingers demanded of him, and that awful tidal wave surging up inside him, out of control once it started, too much all at once, and before he could even get it into her the twitch, the spurt, and her crooked laugh, such a quiet sound that blotted out everything else—and that brought it right back, easy as could be. Oh, he was going to do it, all right, and man, would it ever be exciting!

That was why the mail job was so useful. Had to go to work *so* damn early and he could never get used to waking up before six. But come three o'clock and he was free.

Some afternoons he would go to the movies, hang out in a department store and maybe even buy something. Most afternoons, he would go to the airport. He varied everything: which airport, which route he used. Just to La Guardia alone there were the Train to the Plane, the Carey bus, and about once a month even a taxi. When he got there, sometimes he would waste the trip. Eat Häagen-Dazs cones, a couple of them, and just sit reading the newspaper. At Newark there were a lot of schedules to read and a pretty good bookstore. And if nothing else worked, there was always his little pocket Bible to read. Now, that was the one thing Mom had given him that was any use. It was so soothing to read those familiar-sounding lines over and over again, such a wonderful way of stilling his thoughts. And what better protection could you have against going to hell than to carry a Bible with you everywhere? It was like an amulet. It was magic. It gave him courage. It felt so comforting in his shirt pocket.

Most of the time, he would get right down to business. Check the schedules, pick out a couple of arrivals from likely places— not London or Los Angeles, but smaller places like St. Louis or Topeka. Pick out the arrival gates where the passengers had the longest walk, so he had the most time to look them over. And try not to be at the same gate more often than once a month; he didn't want to be recognized. He thought it would make sense to keep a notebook, but if that were found on him it could mean trouble, premeditation, so he just trusted to memory and luck.

Then, when the passengers started coming, look as if he were searching for someone. She had to be alone, of course, not too large, not too positive-looking. At first he tried to decide on names that seemed to fit them, but that never worked anyway and it was too difficult, so he just picked out a name for the day and stuck with it.

"Are you Carol?" he would say, or "Emily," or "Joan." Never Francesca or Olivia or anything unlikely like that. He knew how small the chances of success were. This plan was going to depend on a lot of patience, a lot of casting bread. "No," she would say, almost every time. Once in a long while, the answer was "Yes," but then he had to say, "I was supposed to meet you," and then the answer was going to be, "But I wasn't expecting anyone." So then he'd have to extricate himself: "Oh, aren't you Carol Martin?" "Why, no," she'd say smiling, and he'd say, "Sorry," and that would be the end of it.

Someday it was all going to click.

Maybe it would be today. Today was going to be one of his serious tries. From the Port Authority Bus Terminal he took the Jersey Transit bus to the Continental terminal at Newark Airport. It was a short trip, and he was there before 4. Continental was a cheapo airline, and Harold thought that made it a likelier place to meet her.

A direct flight from Chicago arrived at 4:20. Harold was there, waiting at the gate as the passengers arrived. But for some reason he knew this flight wouldn't work for him, and he was right; they were mostly men, and the women all looked too purposeful and hard. At 4:45 a flight from Toronto came in. That seemed as though it might be more promising, but no. I'll try at least the next two, he thought, maybe three.

A non-stop from San Francisco landed at 5:05. Harold could see the passengers from a distance, and his interest picked up immediately. There were several women in the bunch, and none of them seemed to be with anybody.

His interest focussed on a woman in a pale green dress. She looked to be in her late twenties, fairly short and slim, carrying a knapsack. Her hair was a brownish red. She was smoking a cigarette, but she seemed bewildered, not quite sure of where she was. So, he tried. As she passed him, he said, "Karen?"

She turned at once and looked at him. "Yes?"

"You're Karen?"

"What else?"

It seemed like a strange reply, but he thought, I don't have to decide anything, just follow the plan. So, feeling his heartbeat, he acted out the scene from memory.

"I'm here to escort you."

"Escort me? What are you talking about?"

"They sent me to bring you in. They didn't want you to have to go by yourself. Seems too dangerous."

She shook her head, shrugged her shoulders. "Sounds peculiar to me. They never sent anyone before."

"I know," said Harold. "It just seems too dangerous for a woman travelling alone. You know, crackheads and all."

"Oh. I see. Who the hell are you, anyway?"

"I'm Harold."

"Well, I don't suppose you're going to make me late."

He'd had his luck, and handled the first part well. But the most difficult part was coming up.

"Get your bags?"

"Naw. This is all I travel with. Can't stand waiting and looking at other people's luggage. Let's just get out of here."

"OK, I'll get the cab."

"*Cab*? Boy, this is *really* a fancy trip. An escort and a cab!"

It was going to work. He could feel the tingle.

They left the terminal and there was the taxi stand, only a couple of cabs waiting. Cabbies must not like Continental, he thought. Passengers too cheap to take cabs and tip right.

This was a crucial moment. He held the door open for her, and after she entered he closed the door and walked around to the other side of the cab, stroking the Bible through his pocket. It was just as he had dreamed it. As he opened his door, she was saying to the cabbie, "155 West 83rd." He couldn't help grinning. Now it didn't matter that he hadn't known where she was heading; she had told him.

He thought about making small talk in the cab, but he had decided that the less he said, the better off he was. Anything he said wrong could expose him. So he tried only a few cautious remarks. "How was the trip?"

"OK."

"Nice, quiet flight, huh?"

"Yeah, just the way I like it."

"Where are you coming from?" he asked.

"I live on Mystery Road, out in San Somewhere."

"Oh," he said with a smile. "And just what do you do out there?"

"In my line of work, you learn not to tell people too much," she said, returning the smile.

She volunteered nothing further and so he sat quietly, just waiting and looking out at the highway. When the cab entered the Lincoln Tunnel, she shivered a bit and moved up to the front of her seat. "These things give me the creeps. I always think the walls are going to collapse and the water will rush in."

"Could happen, I guess, but it never has yet. Not that I know of." She looked at him, smiled, and leaned back in the seat.

As they reached the neighborhood, he felt himself starting to tense up again. He was going to have to handle every step, every remark, very carefully from now on. But before he could say anything, she surprised him with, "Say, it's really early. I could kill an hour or two. You want to join me for a drink?"

He grinned. That couldn't hurt. "Sure," he said. "You know anyplace good?"

"I kind of like the hotel," she said. "It's nice and quiet."

"Fine. Then we'll try the hotel."

As he paid off the cabbie, he did a quick check on the contents of his wallet. He felt confident when he could see the ten hundreds—he thought of them as his getaway money—at the end of the thick wad of bills.

The hotel was right across the street from the building they had been heading for. Karen walked in firmly, leading him without looking back, and Harold followed quietly. The bar was just perfect—spacious, dark, quiet, several comfortable tables. It was too early for a waitress, but they sat right down at a table, Karen depositing her bag on an empty chair. "I'll have a Margarita," she said. "Salt, couple of rocks." Harold walked up to the bar, where the barman looked up lazily. Judging that Karen wouldn't hear him, he ordered her Margarita and a Virgin Mary for himself. Without alcohol his head would be clear.

They sat quietly and sipped their drinks. "God, New York is awful," she said. "The weather here always seems twice as bad as it is anywhere else. If it's hot in San Francisco, it's hot and muggy here. If it's cold in San Francisco, it's snowing here. I can't understand why anybody lives here."

"Neither can I," he said, "and I've always lived here. Hardly ever go anywhere else, and when I do it's always better, but I always come back."

The drinks moved faster than the conversation. She hit bottom just ahead of him.

"Another?" he asked.

"Naw, not this early in the evening," she said. "Well, yeah, sure. Why not? Being in New York is all the excuse I need."

Halfway down the glass, she said, "You know, Harold, you're kind of funny. You don't say much, but you don't leave me wondering, either. It's like I can tell just what you're thinking and you don't have to tell me. That's nice."

He grinned, hoping the grin hid what he was thinking.

"I meet a lot of guys, you know. Guys like me. They think I look nice, you know. So they're always trying to get my attention. They think the thing to do is talk a lot. Some of them ask you a lot of questions, like what a girl wants is to tell you everything. Some of them tell you everything about them, like you're gonna be impressed. This guy on the plane, he was telling me about all his stocks. Hell, like he thought I was gonna jump on his portfolio or something. What a laugh. And this guy I met last week, he was telling me about his three-sports days. It's something new, you know. Go jogging first thing in the morning, then play tennis, then go swimming laps or something. What a joke. But you aren't flapping your mouth so much. I like that. It's nice."

As she looked at him, Harold felt the tingle.

They didn't say anything else until the drinks were finished. Then she said, "I'm gonna be staying here tonight. They don't expect me across the street for a while yet. Why don't you help me get registered."

"Well," said Harold, "I got to be somewhere soon. It's not like I could carry your bags or something." He held his breath.

"Yeah, I know," she said, "but it's more fun having someone you know take you upstairs. Damn bellboys give me the creeps."

Harold exhaled, slowly, cautiously. "Well, OK," he said.

They walked out of the bar, and Harold sat quietly on a chair while Karen walked up to the desk and talked to the clerk.

Soon she walked back to Harold, and he got up and they walked over to the elevator. "Four," she said, and he pushed the buttons. In the elevator, she stood very close to him, not touching but close. He wondered if she noticed his breathing. She handed him the key, and he opened the door for her. She walked in, turned on the light, put her bag down, and sat down on the side of the bed.

"You know, Harold, I get so damn lonely when I come to New York. It's like there's nobody here, just a bunch of faces." She stood up and put her arms around him. He felt her crushing the Bible into his skin.

Now, Harold thought. But his arms wouldn't move. She kissed him on the mouth, and his lips wouldn't move. She giggled and reached around, tickling under his armpit. He gasped, and as his mouth opened she stuck her tongue into it. Harold felt control leave him, and the tingle took over.

"Boy, you're quiet," Karen said. She took his hand and put it on her head. It stroked her hair. She ran her fingers quietly down his back, leaving a tingling trail behind. After a while she stepped away, walked over to the night table beside the bed and turned on the lamp, walked to the entrance to the room and turned off the main light. She walked back to him—he thought she was smiling, but he couldn't really see her face—and carefully took off his shirt and his undershirt. She bent closer and touched her lips to his chest, kissing him lightly, finding the sensitive places. Then she stepped back a step, seemed to shrug and shiver, and her dress fell around her. Her hands went behind her, and her bra came loose and she shook her shoulders and it fell also. Still standing a step away, she reached out and began to stroke him, all over at once it seemed. Sweat ran down Harold's forehead into his eyes and his mouth. His hands began to move on their own. Karen threw back her head and sighed, then took his hand in hers and led him towards the bed. But he seemed to have missed something, because his pants and shoes were off too. And she was touching him again, and the tingle was overwhelming, but it was somehow different than he remembered. Something was making his body move, but he didn't know what it was. He was so dizzy that if he had been standing he would have fallen, but he wasn't standing, just moving, up and down, like push-ups, he thought. And this time, when the tidal wave started, it was just right, and he heard someone moaning and gasping but he didn't know if it was him or her or both of them, and as the explosion came he saw a blinding light that wiped away everything, even though his eyes were closed.

He couldn't say anything, but he began to cry softly. I can't believe it, he thought. It was just like I always wanted. She held him tightly against her, making quiet little noises, until finally he rolled just a little bit away from her, noticing that he was on top of the bed cover as he drifted into a dreamless sleep.

When Harold awoke, it was very dark in the room, only a sliver of light coming in under the door, but he knew immediately where he was. He felt around for the lamp, turned it on. He knew at once that Karen was gone, even before he saw his clothing neatly arranged on the chair. "She had to go," he said out loud, but he smiled. He looked at his watch and was surprised to see that it was after ten. He dressed slowly, looking around the room. Then he sat on the chair for a while, just looking.

Finally he got up. He turned the table lamp off, then turned it back on and left the room. In the elevator, he started to whistle. He looked at the desk clerk as he left the building.

He walked down the street, heading for the subway. At the street corner where the station was, a man approached him, tall, wearing a torn shirt and pants of no color, with floppy shoes and no socks. "I won't lie to you, buddy," he said. "All I want is a bottle of wine. Can you help me out?"

"Sure," said Harold. "I won't be needing this any more." He reached into his pocket, pulled out his wallet, and took the wad of bills out of it. It seemed thinner than it should have been, but he hardly even noticed long enough to wonder where the rest had gone. He took the first single, saying, "I'll need a token," and handed the rest to the panhandler without looking at them. "You'll be needing this even more," he added. He reached into his pocket, pulled out the Bible, and handed that over too. Then, whistling to himself, he walked down the stairs to the train.

❖

Splinter From True Guitar
Scott Morgan

LEGENDS OF MASTER

There was a child. At his birth celestial harmonies were heard.
He played guitar when he turned thirteen. In mudbrick town
on low border he created sounds never heard before. All
saviors had been forgotten. Poor and humbled were massed on
low border, every dark one, had least of everything. Power,
comfort, wealth were in northland, dreamed of as paradise by
those on low border. Wealth didn't help people of northland.
Their kingtowns were crumbling, plague in walls, wires,
screens, chips. Many from northland were turning into Radi-
ants, eaten by disease, dying at earlier and earlier ages. One
day a man, a woman, a child would be fine, then they shriveled
and died. Master played, he said

> Our souls exist in separate rooms,
> puffed up like balloons.
> Disease hit, pop balloon soul,
> it shrivel, body shrivel with it.
> Nothing left but sack of skin,
> bones disintegrating at slightest touch.
> Need a strong soul to survive.
> Come from a hard life.

When Master played crowds cried and screamed, churned
their bodies, strings of Master's guitar like strings of their souls.
Each time he touched a string people felt something pull at
their souls. Couldn't help it. Some wanted to destroy Master,
destroy his guitar. Too much power, they were afraid to have
him play their hearts, their souls.

When Master played he was very aware, totally conscious. Played people until their strength was drained, until they opened their eyes. Played, and many wanted to turn World Corporation upside down. They cried, "Why can't we eat, drink? Why we have no space for ourselves?" Master played, space inside people opened up, great open fields, lush, fruitful, enough room for ten generations in each person.

Master had cleft lip. Master couldn't speak like men. He played, interpreter turned music to words for Master.

Master had shape of teardrop in his eyes. So much light in his eyes he saw what no one else could.

Leaders scared. One Corporation, ten leaders, controlled everything. Sky shimmered at night with bright specks, stations of control, called by Corporation stations of delight. Sent pictures into people's minds, visions of northland—beautiful objects, houses of colored glass, beautiful faces, bodies, possibilities. People of low border saw beautiful pictures, they forgot hunger, thirst. Light dulled in their eyes while they were dreaming of paradise, dreaming of northland. Master played, pictures dissolved. Music of Master cut right into people. He played, pictures dissolved. Leaders turned scared. They said, "This has never happened before," and tried to buy Master.

Master was small and dark, bones for shoulders, body like a stick. Sometimes he jerked like a puppet, looked spastic, people wondered, "Can this be Master?" Guitar in his hands, many were convinced. See his fingers? Each one look like a person, each one have a personality. Each finger have eyes.

Where did Master learn to play? Did Master have a teacher? Who could teach Master?

It was said

Old man come to window of baby Master, play one note over and over. Everyone say, Wind. He come again, play two notes. Everyone say, Trees creaking. He come again, no one see him.

Hear that sound? Maybe an animal. Maybe a bird. All night, sound play outside window. All day, sound echoing in baby Master's room. Master have a mother. She listen. Her eyes be burning, she have a face like fire when sound swallow room. Friends see her, they moan. Sound in room enter them, tear their souls, like cat sewn in belly.

It was said

Old man once seen near shack. He looked like mud, no clothes, looked 100, 200, 300 years old. Carried something on his bent back. What was it? Nobody know. Later, when Master reveal himself, everyone say, "I saw old man." Say, Old man father of Master." When Master hear it he howl, laugh like a madman. Say, "I like that story."

How did Master get his True Guitar?
It was said

When Master turn thirteen violent storm roll across land. Stations of control sputter in sky, pictures in minds turn dim, fade. Everyone terrified, they cry, "Now comes our end!" One full day and night, everywhere. Then it stop. Just like that. Sun come out, it shine like a beautiful face. Moon slice through clouds, night look like day. Everyone thankful, rejoicing everywhere. Night of Long Storm over! A miracle. Who know why?

Outside Master's shack stand ancient tree, planted in beginning of time. Bolt of lightning strike that tree, carve it up. Nothing left but True Guitar. Master just add strings.

Some shook their heads at story, said, "Not possible." Said, "Old mud man give Master guitar carried on his bent back." Others asked them, "Where mud man find True Guitar?" They had no answer, and there was no one to ask.

Where did Master first reveal himself?
After Night of Long Storm, Master, just turned thirteen, journeyed to Angel-In-Hand to hear Ebentide, king of guitar, play in his Club Callou.

Everyone knew Ebentide. Powerful man. Hands wide as wings. Ebentide would spread himself huge on stage of pleasure in Club Callou. Behind him hornmen would sweat and blow, pulse of drums rumbled. Walls of ancient corrugated steel shivered with sound, never stopped ringing. Spinners and shakers, hungry and humbled, travelled from every corner of low border region to hear man of great power play his guitar. Came to him by tens, by hundreds, by thousands. What Ebentide offered no one else could. What he did with his guitar no one else knew how.

Those were days of Ebentide, in his glory.

He stood on platform, huge guitar hidden behind hands wide as wings, smile of great persuasion on his massive copper face. When Ebentide laughed it was like roll of thunder. Spinners and shakers broke their hearts in happiness, burned together, loins to loins. Hungry and humbled were witless with pleasure. House of Ebentide rocked day and night. They cried his name in their ecstasies,

"Ebentide! Ebentide!"

Ebentide knew magic. He played, everyone forgot sorrow. They said, "See Ebentide. In his vast joy there no room for sorrow." Leaders of Corporation were pleased. They needed this man of joy and forgetting, said, "Let him play. While he plays, we are safe."

No one controlled Ebentide. He played pure, joy so pure for Ebentide he felt agonies of joy in his music. It was life itself to him. When crowds pressed into Club Callou Ebentide drew pleasure from them, swelled on stage, looked like a king, some said a god. He played guitar by night, played it by day. Spinners and shakers came, he gave them release. They cried, wailed, spinning and shaking, felt drunk, hot, rolled with each other in dirt, crying, "Ebentide! Ebentide!"

Ebentide knew sorrow. Knew poor, sick, humbled entered Club Callou to listen, to forget. Pictures from stations of control not always enough to comfort these. Ebentide pushed people with his music, saw an edge, just where most players stopped, only Ebentide pushed them further, played music that overwhelmed remembering, because that was where greatest joy appeared to Ebentide, over an edge where remembering stopped.

After Night of Long Storm, Club Callou was filled to every inch of its huge space. Streets of Angel-In-Hand, covered with mud washed down from hills, were dense with jubilant crowds come in their joy and thankfulness to hear Ebentide play. Hornmen wailed. Pulse of drums rumbled. Ebentide played so rich, Club Callou couldn't contain his music. It burst like a flood through Angel-In-Hand, covered countryside, reached small dark boy alone on road after midnight, led him straight to Club Callou. Boy passed between spinners and shakers, no one noticed him except Ebentide. He saw a boy moving slowly towards platform, small, dark, dirty with mud, carrying guitar on his back. Cleft lip. Pupils of eyes shaped like teardrops. Walked with head cocked to side, squinting up.

Ebentide stared at boy, heard a sound pulsing from him, tried to disregard it, played to his people, loud, fast, fierce. Spinners and shakers howled with pleasure, sick and humbled rocked their bodies in delight, but all that time Ebentide heard a wilder sound, a sound without limits, a sound that was like entering a cave. Two steps in and Ebentide was lost in that sound, a sound like a cave that had no end, opening towards him from small dark boy. Ebentide cried in himself, "Who is this child?"

For first time, Ebentide was pierced by sound he didn't create, so startled he stopped playing. Horns ceased. Drums were held between their beat. Everyone was silent, wondering what happened to Ebentide.

Ebentide motioned to boy standing in crowd. Boy stepped forward and climbed onto platform, squinting up, smiling his crooked smile. Ebentide pointed to guitar on his back, said, "You play." Everyone squealed with laughter, cried, "Can little boy play music of man?"

Boy said no word, let his thin brown fingers speak on strings, and no one laughed.

> You souls in flight,
> spin and shake to forget.
> What will that serve?
> Better to remember.
> You dancing in cages.
> Call that life?
> Happy in a cage?

Those were words Ebentide heard in his heart, listening to Master's music. Music spoke words inside Ebentide. He shook with terror. What boy was this? Small dark child, cleft lip, teardrop eyes, playing sounds Ebentide himself, king of guitar, never heard before? Couldn't be just a boy, must be spirit from somewhere. When anyone asked Ebentide in his later days, "How you first know Master was Master?" he repeated those words, heard in his heart.

Music of Master hit spinners and shakers, sick and humbled like a fierce north wind, like a cold salt wave. He played and played until music broke through cages, straight into their hearts. Crowds turned angry. Sounds of Master were like no music ever heard before. They felt trapped, rushed towards platform, eyes bloodwild, screaming, howling, "You, boy, what you know! You can't play music. Get off! Go home!" Inside they were sweating, frightened, outside in anger they tried to drown out Master's sounds.

Master stopped playing. Squinted at crowd head cocked, curious, surprised, but not angry at all. He giggled. Crowd fell back. Master pointed to Ebentide's huge guitar, held in limp hands. Ebentide refused to play it.

"Why play?" he asked Master, trembling, copper eyes gleaming. "I heard what I should."

Master shook his head, smiled his crooked smile. Looked like a puppet next to massive Ebentide.

"You play," Master told him, sputtering, pulling each word from cleft mouth like words were twisted roots of trees. "Your time still."

Ebentide wanted to leave Club Callou just then and follow Master. He said, "No one to follow anymore. I follow you."

Master asked, "If I give you note, that be enough?"

Ebentide told him, "I play that note till you return."

Master shrugged his thin shoulders. "If I do."

How Master Got His Cleft Lip

Everyone know, before each soul enters human form, packed tight in seven pounds of child, it is taken on a tour. Tour guides on high, messengers of Highest, lead soul this way and that, one end of universe to other, exposing mysteries. Then, just as soul, crammed with knowledge, is about to settle into child, tour guide hits soul in its face, just on upper lip. Makes soul forget everything before it enters world. Gives soul a reason to be born. Why come into life if soul know everything already? Or, why live if there is nothing already given, nothing to be remembered? Mark of messenger is little indentation on upper lip, right in middle. Everyone has it. Why do babies cry when they enter world? It is their souls in tears, sting of messenger fingers still on new flesh, remembering for last time how much they must now forget.

When Master's soul prepare to descend, his messenger greets Master politely, says, Let me take you once more around. Then Master is given Grand Tour, every secret place, every trick of creation, mystery of mysteries, harmony of heaven. It is important to Highest that Master know even last secret sound of universe before he forget. When Grand Tour is concluded messenger, still very polite, says, Pardon me, it is my duty, and gently tries to lay his hand on Master. Master ducks. Messenger swings again. Master dips, bobs, weaves. Master refuse to forget anything! Other messengers come running. Such a thing never happen before. They cry in despair, cascade of pearls falling from their eyes. They plead with Master, No one goes down knowing everything. Master don't care. Then his messenger says in sorrow, What they will do to me for my failure! Master, full of compassion, declares, Strike as you please, I am descending. His messenger, rushed, fearful, swings hard but off center. Rips Master's face. Pain forms teardrops that never leave his eyes. Master is born with cleft lip, but secret of secrets, harmony of harmonies, is still his.

Night after Master left Angel-In-Hand Ebentide gazed at masses below him from stage of Club Callou, believed, Now is time to play Master's note. Bodies of spinners and shakers were coiled tight, expectant. Sick, humbled listened silently for music that would release them, make them forget. Ebentide, in glory of his full power, and with Master's words, "Your time still," in his heart, told hornmen and drummen to wait. He covered strings of his guitar with his huge hands, played Master's note. No one moved, no one made a sound. Ebentide drove that note straight for their hearts. Everyone listened, no one moved. He floated note above them like man on a trapeze, spun it, rolled it, curled it like smoke, used that note like a whip, lashed it.

Crowds below stayed silent, looked up at him respectful, but not shocked, frightened, like when they heard Master play. Ebentide played his note in every progression, tried to pound cage of each person's heart, shatter it by his full strength. Then Ebentide heard a sound. Laughter. From one, then many. Spinners and shakers moved slow, then faster and faster, riotous, screaming and laughing at this great joke Ebentide offered them.

Ebentide howled, great god face sweating, gleaming. He wrestled with that note, tried to make it sound like Master, but it belonged to Ebentide. Hornmen wailed through their horns, drums crashed like buildings falling. Ebentide played and played, suddenly saw himself as puppetman, controlling strings to arms, legs, loins of spinners and shakers, twisting below him, bodies jerking madly. Through huge metal doors opened to outside, where music filled streets of Angel-In-Hand, Ebentide saw crowds rolling in mud, heard rising thunder of his name roared from them in their great joy,

Ebentide! Ebentide!

Ebentide moaned. Was that all his music could bring? Idiot laughter? Bodies rolling in mud? He played Master's note desperate, cut his fingers, blood making strings squeak and stick. Crowd didn't care. Shouted his name over and over, beating their hearts, rocking and moaning, spinning and shaking. Then Ebentide knew it was hopeless. Couldn't play one note of Master's music like Master, couldn't touch souls of crowds. Knew he must wait, play as he could. Time had not come for Master yet. It was Ebentide's time still.

Such were middle days of Ebentide, full of bitterness.

Ebentide changed after he heard Master. Man of great joy and forgetting turned mean, brooding. Every day before dusk Ebentide wandered alone to edge of town, where even meagrest hut, bush stopped. If someone tried to follow him Ebentide howled, forced that person back. Spinners and shakers shook their heads, asked, "What he looking for at edge of town, alone, where desert begin?"

Every day after sun died, and stations shined brightly in jet sky, Ebentide returned to Club Callou, played his music, wilder, fiercer than ever. If people asked, "Ebentide, what you waiting for?" he cried in anger, "You fools not to know!"

Three years passed, to Ebentide like decades. Anger always in his glazed eyes. Did Ebentide sleep? Each day he stood where desert began, each night he played, in his heart waiting for Master to return. Bitter he did not come. Then bitter he came at all.

Ebentide still played Master's note inside his own music, every variation. Couldn't play note out of himself, couldn't play self out of note. Lost in a cave.

No one played with Ebentide now. Musicians listened with fear and wonder to an Ebentide they never heard before. Spinners and shakers, sick, lame, humbled still filled Club Callou to be released, to forget. Ebentide felt no more joy in them, lost even sorrow, pity. Everywhere he looked saw people happy in their blindness, saw every soul locked in a cage. No pleasure left to Ebentide. Not even music brought pleasure. Only bitterness.

When Master returned he found Ebentide at edge of town, sun dying, stations of control twinkling in sky. Ebentide said, "Why did you wait? It too late now."

Master smiled his crooked smile. "Been busy."

Master carried his guitar, wood blond, strings simple steel. Ebentide said, "Play for me."

Master played, small dark body rocking back and forth. Ebentide heard those sounds as words, speaking inside him. Heard them as though Master himself was speaking.

> Child born, he is king.
> It is majesty of new life.
> Everyone seek tiny child's approval,
> fawn over child.
> Child don't care. You of child's realm?
> What can you offer him?
> He already king of his new kingdom.
> Child turn older, seek approval. No one have time.
> Child say, Listen to me. How many listen?

I play newborn, it is my kingdom.
You listen or not, I care?
Still you treat me like king.
I play to you as older child, say, Listen to me!
cry, scream, beg, you shut your ears, say,
We hear this before.
Child from womb is like man from dead.
Everyone in their heart say, Tell us,
have you remembered? What are your secrets?
Until child have words, mysteries remain.
With first word, child leave his kingdom,
become lowest in your realm.

All hope for mysteries disappear.

What can I say you haven't already heard?
My words same as yours.

Ebentide brooded over Master's words, heard in his heart. He repeated them for Master, asked, "These words yours?"

Master put down his guitar, shrugged.

Ebentide said, "Your sounds scare people. Maybe they hear your words. Let me speak your words for you."

Master pointed to his cleft lip, said, "Not made for words anyway."

What Master Was Like As A Child

One day Master play outside. Just a boy, six years old. Mother of Master hear CrackCrackCrack. She run outside, see Master in mud, on all fours, head down. Suddenly he lift his hands, bring two rocks together, CrackCrackCrack. Master laugh wildly, "Rocks singing!" Mother scream, "Get out of mud. You look like animal!" Master cock his head to mother. Then he cry. Open his cleft mouth and cry. No sound come out, but mother hear cry in her bones. Master cry and cry, don't seem to breathe, cry pouring from him. Mother hear it in every cell of her body, hear every cry inside it, every sorrow, misery, pain. She hear cry of rock, tree, water, air, how they sick, how they suffer. Mother break down and cry, tears and wailing. Master close his mouth and look at her, head bent almost upside down, say to her, "I stop, now you stop too." She cry and cry and cry.

Ebentide followed Master, no one knew where. House of Ebentide, Club Callou, was silent. Musicians waited. Spinners and shakers waited. Poor and humbled waited. Every day they expected Ebentide. Crowds came, filled Angel-In-Hand, no one left. They said, "When he return he play us into new ecstasies. He gathering power." Fever of excitement spread through town. Everyone waited.

Months passed. Earth burned brown, then black. Iridescence of trees drained out.

Spinners and shakers began to say, "He never return." A few left, then many followed. Time had come for Dreams Made Real in desert city of desires, built in deepest valley just below border to northland. Border was walled and wired, patrolled by Paradise Troopers. Few from low border region thought of entering northland.

What was Dreams Made Real?

One week each year Corporation had a celebration. Only those from low border could come, be given every satisfaction, food, drink, anything they wanted. Beautiful men and women from northland, bodies in bright cloth, faces painted, offered pleasure in every variation to crowds. Empty buildings of colored glass sparkled like jewels. Wheels of lights revolved above huts of white clay, bleached stone. At gates to city stood two steel wings, fifty feet high. Sunlight hit them, they shimmered and gleamed, looked alive, like whole city of desires be carried aloft. Stations of control burned at their brightest, raced pictures through minds, beautiful dreams of one week to hold crowds throughout year.

Corporation called it Dreams Made Real. Even poorest of poor could have every pleasure there, even those who could not come were happy with possibility, knew next year they would have their chance again. People of low border believed everyone had this life in northland. Corporation told them, "One day this life will be yours too."

In center of desert city high platform was filled with musicians from northland and low border. City was crowded beyond edge of desert, everyone listening. Master and Ebentide were pressed tight in crowd, not far from platform.

106

Ebentide stood hunched, head bowed, wrapped in huge cloak so no one would know him. Master listened to musicians, smiled his crooked smile, applauded loud as anyone. Ebentide wanted to destroy city of desires, burn it to ash, mix ash with dust of desert, so even desert would forget city of desires was once built there. He told Master, "They destroying souls of our people. Every picture, every pleasure, every sound they play. Sounds I once played."

Master laughed, took his guitar hidden under Ebentide's cloak, played one note, two. Everything stopped. No one saw who played note, because Master was small beyond noticing, but note rippled through crowd, radiated out, even those beyond edge of city heard it, felt it in their bones. Nothing could be clearer than that sound, echoing inside each person. Beautiful pictures began to melt. Pleasures seemed smaller and smaller, until those pleasures disappeared. Without pictures, pleasures, there was only nakedness, so sudden people cried and moaned. But there was handful in crowd who cried for pure joy of sudden nakedness inside of them.

Master played his music on True Guitar, notes, chords, progressions of sounds never heard before. Ebentide dropped his cloak and stood huge, copper face gleaming. Many in crowd recognized Ebentide's face, thought he was playing. Music of Master spoke in Ebentide's heart. He spoke as Master played, but it was not voice of Ebentide

You frightened without pictures.
What good are pictures?
When you leave, is that your life?
How many still sick, hungry?
When you dream, whose dreams you dream?
Can't even dream your own dreams.

Better to be naked.
Better to forget pictures.
Then comes remembering.
Before you born you had a soul.
Soul shown universe.
Soul shown mysteries.
Your souls scared now.
Frightened souls, souls in hiding,
little souls like ghosts, puffs of smoke.

Souls need room.
Yours smothered by false pictures.
Listen!
Even these words give false pictures.
Better to forget them. Just listen.

Delegates of Corporation were frightened. They told leaders, "A boy was here, played sounds on his guitar never heard before."

Leaders said, "It is nothing to us."

Delegates told them, "No one escapes his sounds. When he played everything else stopped. His sounds passed through everything, into everyone, couldn't be drowned out. Burned away all pictures we sent."

Leaders asked, "What does he offer instead?"

They said, "He offers nothing. A feeling of nothing, of nakedness."

Leaders laughed, "Should we fear a boy who offers nothing?" They had no time to think of small dark child who played guitar. Even delegates did not know how fast radiant disease was spreading through kingtowns of northland.

Delegates said, "People were talking to each other. We heard them ask, Are Dreams Made Real our dreams?"

Leaders asked, "Was he alone?"

Delegates said, "Ebentide was with him, speaking to crowds. People listened."

Leaders said, "We will buy this boy."

When Master left desert city of desires, travelling south to Angel-In-Hand, two were followers of Master. One was Ebentide. Other was young as Master, short, had shocked white hair, milk skin, no eyebrows, black lenses in his glasses, eyes no one could see. Wore a long black coat, wore a guitar string around his neck, looped twice. Name was Praelot. He praised music of Master. Whispered to Master, "You are unique. Your music can bring you anything. I can help."

Master laughed like a wildman, like a jackal. "Anything?"

Milkwhite man said "Yes."

Master said, "Time comes, I ask."

That night Ebentide woke Master, told him, "This one not of

us. Wants money, control, maybe sent by Corporation. Others just like him come to Club Callou, beg for my music, make every promise. Only want music for power, control. You need this one? He will sell you."

Master smiled his crooked smile, said very slowly, every word slow and painful to hear, "Must have thing to sell before he can sell. My sounds? Already out, in air, in his bones, can have it free. Maybe I tell him that. Have it free. Anyone. Him. You. Have it free."

End Of Part 1

"Legends Of Master" is Part 1 of "Splinter from True Guitar." Part 2 is "Chronicles of Master in Angel-In-Hand." Part 3 is "When Master Entered History."

The Rooster and the Rummage Sale

Jo McKim Chalmers

Don't get the impression that I am addicted to yard or rummage sales. On the contrary, I am usually at home cooking, cleaning, or pulling up weeds in the garden. Sometimes I write a few words.

But for many Woodstockers (second-home owners, summer residents, and tourists) rummaging has become a weekend sport, a treasure, a scavenger hunt. They fan out over the countryside, local newspapers in hand, even crossing the Hudson River. Eventually some of them will hold yard sales of their own, when the fruits of their rummaging threaten to overrun their dwellings.

This particular week, feeling more indolent and irresponsible than usual, I skipped the "Letters to the Editor" in the *Woodstock Times* and turned to the classifieds, where under Yard Sales was listed a Moving Sale, with an address on Plochmann Lane—one of the better Lanes for that sort of thing, its occupants seeming to have acquired a more interesting range of objects and to be less loath to part with them for a reasonable sum. At least, that has been my experience.

Of course, some who advertise a Moving Sale have no intention of going anywhere except to their own backyard, where they will display a motley collection of faded, warped, bent, and shrunken bits of jetsam. They will then lie in wait for a pack rat to come along and relieve them of enough of it — before it rains—to pay for the ad in the *Woodstock Times*.

However, that is the exception. With any luck, you may find the perfect gift for someone who has "everything." Then tuck it away until the holidays or a birthday. Exchanging presents with a fellow rummager can also be full of surprises.

In the lives of the people who are holding the sale, unique, amusing, even antique objects can be found. I have unearthed,

110

for example, a real scorpion embedded in a glass paperweight; a painting of a lone wolf trekking through a snowing wilderness, mounted in a wide black frame which makes the wolf appear even more desolate; long-ago books, poignantly illustrated; fabulous costume jewelry; cow bells; little rag dolls with smudged faces; and a longed-for oak steamer chair, in mint condition, for a pittance.

I arrived in the late afternoon of the final day of the Moving Sale on Plochmann Lane. If an antique dealer hasn't picked the sale clean before dawn of the first day, this can sometimes be an opportune time to attend. If the occupants of the house are actually moving somewhere, they will have greatly reduced the price of the remaining *accumulatio*, so as to avoid exclaiming later—when unpacking, say on the West Coast—"Now, why did I ever bring that!"

I really shouldn't have gone to the sale. I was temporarily short of cash...but maybe I'd find some little thing.

The house on Plochmann Lane looked like a modern version of the Witch's gingerbread house in *Hansel and Gretel.* And on the lawn, erect and alert, stood a handsomely feathered rooster who, as I stepped out of the car, went aloft and headed in my direction. I jumped back into my car, rolled up the window, and tapped discreetly on the horn. A tall, shiny-haired, attractive young woman, dressed in old jeans and a faded blue work shirt, appeared. She picked up the rooster, scolded him with a raised finger, took him into the house, reappeared, apologized for his behavior, and assured me of safe passage.

When we entered the kitchen, the cock was perched on the top of an opened door which led to the upstairs. The woman laughed. "He's a household pet," she explained. She removed him from his perch, tossed him on the stairs, and closed the door.

I looked around. There wasn't much left, but I could do with a few more stainless steel forks, and found three which almost matched my own. Then I came upon a large spoon which had in its center a small, mesh sort-of window. Instantly I fell in love with it. It wasn't just another kitchen utensil turned out by some factory or other. It had been *created*; it had a Modern Museum look about its well-formed, bright yellow handle; and its little hinged mesh window would capture every bit—and properly drain it—of the white of a whirled-poached egg. I desperately wanted that spoon, but had only a bit of change left. Surely not enough.

"How much?" I asked. "It's lovely."

"Take it," the young woman said. "I'm sure no one else is coming this late."

"Oh, no," was my answer.

"Please take it," she urged. "Otherwise it will only end up at the Library Fair."

Being even temporarily out of cash can shade one's response to the opportunities of life and keep one from rising to them like a trout to the fly (the real fly-around fly, that is). I wanted that darling spoon with all my heart. And yet, I didn't answer "I'd love it. Thank you very much." No. Instead, with a total lack of grace, I answered, "I'm sorry. I can't accept it." How very unkind of me that was. The sweet lady wanted me to have it. And that spoon couldn't wait to go home with me. I know it couldn't.

Sure enough, they were driving west. "What will you do with the rooster?" I inquired on my way out.

"We're giving him to a friend."

"A friend?!" I exclaimed.

"Oh, he's forewarned," she assured me. "He's looking forward to the challenge." She opened the stair door and gathered the bird to her.

"Have a safe trip," I said.

She held the rooster in her arms until I had reached my car, then tossed him into the air and waved me good-bye.

Someday at a rummage sale—it may be years from now— I feel I will find that spoon again. Even if by then its little mesh window is pierced and rusted, I will grasp it firmly and take it home where it belongs.

❖

Najmeh

Maria Bauer

BEBACHSHIT, DASHUI KOJAST?—(Excuse me, where is the washroom?)

DAR ANJOMAN IRANO-EMRIKA'ST.—(It is in the Irano-American Society.)

We, a small group of foreign service officers' wives recently arrived in Tehran, were dutifully repeating the sentences of the Persian lessons which the State Department's Foreign Service Institute had devised. That we were not bored to tears was entirely due to Najmeh Ashgar, our teacher, who held our complete attention. With her large black eyes and jet black hair contrasting with her porcelain-white skin, she had the characteristic features of a beautiful young Persian woman. There was a glow about her, an animation and enthusiasm that completely captivated us. She obviously enjoyed teaching us and somehow managed to enliven these idiotic dialogues with amusing, typically Persian idioms in order to convey to us the special flavor of her language.

"May your shadow never grow less" (May you remain healthy) and "May your nose grow fat" (May you become prosperous), she wished us when our four weeks' course came to an end. I had barely learned a few sentences and was eager to continue studying, but in the only way I am capable of learning a language, namely through grammar and written exercises. Najmeh was delighted with my decision and agreed to give me private lessons.

This was in 1958, still under the Shah, when the mountains surrounding Tehran had not yet disappeared behind a veil of pollution; when bicycles, donkey carts, sheep and turkeys still competed with cars on the dusty streets and the city was not yet overrun by foreigners as it would be later in the years preceding the Islamic Revolution.

113

Three times a week I would go to Najmeh's small house on Naderi Street where, like a child, I started filling the lines of a notebook with the letters of the Persian alphabet. It had always fascinated me. Ever since our arrival, a one-word sign in beautiful calligraphy had particularly intrigued me. It appeared everywhere—over food stores or coffee shops, painted on trees and even in huge white letters on the rock of a far-away mountain. It was a tremendous feeling of triumph when, after a few lessons, I was able to decipher it. It said COCA COLA.

We worked with great concentration during these lessons for which Najmeh refused to be paid. When I protested, she used to say, "But Maria, I enjoy them so. How can I charge for something I enjoy doing?" Later I often wondered whether she ever realized that these lessons and our hours of conversation by far transcended the language—that they became my key to an understanding of her country and a growing fondness for it at a time when I was still suffering acutely from culture shock.

Soon my interest shifted from the language to Najmeh, who kept revealing new, entirely unexpected facets of her personality. At first, I was only struck by her independence, quite unusual for an Iranian woman at that time. When she was not busy giving classes to Americans, she kept inviting illiterate workers or garbage collectors to her house, where she taught them to read and write despite her husband's vigorous protests.

"But Reza," I once heard her say to him, "how can I, in good conscience, teach foreigners our language when so many of our own people cannot even read and write?"

Najmeh never allowed any interruptions during classes, but when Leila, her five-year-old daughter, burst into the room, her interest in the lessons immediately vanished. Leila, her black curls and glowing eyes peering out of her tiny round face, was devoid of any shyness and could be quite a nuisance, but Najmeh seemed helpless as she watched her child's every move with infinite affection.

After our lessons Najmeh always served Turkish coffee and when we finished drinking it she made me hold my tiny cup upside down on the saucer for a while and then she would read my fortune from the design the grounds made on the bottom of my cup. Her characterizations of me and her predictions were amazing. Nejmeh's antennae were so sensitive that she would be aware of things I had on my mind without my ever having mentioned them. And soon over these empty cups of coffee, in her fluent and melodious English, she would reveal to me, bit by bit, her thoughts and her agonizing aspirations and frustrations.

In the beginning her intense personality and her totally different background were so alien to me that I was reluctant to walk into the intimacy of her private life; but she eagerly reached out and opened up to me without the slightest inhibition, as though she wanted to test her anxieties and intuitions on someone who was a complete outsider in her culture.

"All my life I had to fight for or against something," she once told me when she reminisced about her childhood. "I wanted to go to school with girls of my own age, but no, I had to stay home and take lessons with an old *mullah*. And when I knew how to read and write, instead of being taught the subjects I was becoming interested in, I had to memorize parts of the Koran because that was as far as the *mullah's* knowledge went. Then I had to fight to go to high school and to stay until graduation because my parents felt that this was all the education I would need since I would soon be married anyway. And when I was married, I had to fight Reza for so many things...."

Reza, an engineer in his mid-thirties, only a few years older than Najmeh, was a nice-looking, rather meek man who continually seemed torn between anger and admiration for his wife's unorthodox behavior. Although the marriage had been arranged, Najmeh was now obviously in love with him, but she stuck to her convictions even though they were quite contrary to his conservative opinions. After her marriage she took English and education courses at Tehran University to prepare her for a teaching career. Insisting that she and Reza move into a home of their own, she managed to free herself from the influence of her mother-in-law; that alone was a revolutionary attitude in a tribal society. And she never gave up rebelling against the fact that Reza had a mistress on the side, a custom few wives at the time thought of fighting. After all, in the Moslem world a man is still entitled to four wives, and although in those days few educated Iranian men took advantage of that tradition, taking a *singhe* (concubine) was still generally accepted. But the greatest crisis arose when Najmeh converted to Catholicism and insisted on having Leila baptized too, so that she would not have to suffer the humiliations of a Moslem woman. From then on, Najmeh was completely shunned by Reza's family and friends.

"Wasn't it a difficult decision to break with Islam?" I asked her.

"Of course, it was awful. I used to be a very good Moslem child, or rather a very religious child. I was always interested in other religions and couldn't quite see why there was such a fuss about what kind of religion people had as long as they believed in one God. Christianity attracted me. Or perhaps it was the mystical atmosphere of the Catholic churches. I loved to read about saints and their miracles. But, since I happened to have been born a Moslem, I accepted that Mohammad was the greatest of the prophets and that Islam was the only true faith."

"What made you change your mind? Was it before or after your marriage?"

"Oh, long before. It all started after an experience...but never mind, it happened a long time ago."

"You'd rather not talk about it?"

There was a moment of silence as Najmeh stared into the distance and then, suddenly, she threw her head back and laughed. "Well, all right, I'll tell you. It's a terrible story; but it will help you understand....

"I must have been about 12 years old when Father took me, during the Moharram holidays, on a pilgrimage to Meshed. On the way he told me all the details about the martyrdom of Hussein and Ali, how they shed their blood for their faith and about the sufferings of their followers. In Meshed we spent hours circling the Holy Shrine, squeezed among crowds of men who were crying and beating themselves with chains until blood was running down their backs and chests. There was something catching about that despair and the rhythm of their flagellations, so I too started to beat my chest with my fists; but father stopped me, saying that girls were not supposed to do that. Then we prayed at the tomb of Iman and I cried and cried—the whole thing was a tremendously emotional experience.

"When we finally got to the hotel where we were to spend

116

the night, I was filled with religious fervor but totally exhausted and hysterical from all that crying. In my room I felt faint; my knees were trembling and my thighs were moist. Having no idea of the facts of life, I was startled to see blood dripping down my legs—deep red blood like that shed by Ali and Hussein and by all those men at the shrine—and yet there was no wound and no pain at all. I was convinced that this was a miracle. I was bleeding for the martyrs—the proof that I was a Moslem and that Islam was the true faith."

"Did you tell your father?"

"No, but back home the next day I told Mother. She explained that 'miracle' to me, probably in more detail than I was prepared to hear. And then she told me about the pain of conceiving and childbearing, about the duty of total submission to all of one's husband's wishes. That, according to Allah and his Prophet, is the one role of a good Moslem woman. Now that I had become a woman, she said, I would have to wear the *chador* and soon she and Father would start looking for a proper husband.

"I was appalled, and so disillusioned. This was when the worst fighting with my parents started. I refused to wear the veil. I refused the many matches my parents were trying to arrange for me. I still believed in Islam but I felt that Mohammad's teachings had been in some ways misunderstood and misinterpreted. Later I was convinced that we, the modern educated generation, would be able to change people's attitudes. But that, of course, was an illusion because the power and influence of the *mullahs* is still too strong. Even now I believe that Mohammad would have understood the necessity for change; but the *mullahs* don't."

"So your conversion was really a rebellion against Islam?"

"Oh, no, that alone would not have decided me. I had the same conflict so many of our modern women have these days: on the one hand they want independence and a good education, and on the other hand they want to be good Moslems. But apparently you cannot have both, not yet at least. So those who choose equality and freedom will go after it and not take Islam very seriously anymore. But I had to know more, more about what was right and what the meaning of it all was, and I kept searching, and all that time I was drawn more and more to Catholicism by so many signs. The revelations I found in the scriptures, the deep faith that overwhelmed me in church, holding me warm and secure—all that convinced me that Catholicism would give me the answer or peace of mind or whatever it is one calls 'grace.'"

Najmeh was not always in a mood for philosophical discussions; sometimes she displayed a wonderful enjoyment of life while involving herself almost childishly in material concerns. There were days when we explored the city together, going on shopping expeditions where she would spend extravagant amounts of money on make-up, clothes and trinkets. And both of us loved to lose ourselves in the labyrinth of oriental confusion by driving—amid the deafening noise of cars and trucks blowing their horns at flocks of scared sheep, donkeys and excitable pedestrians, past rows of old, sad-looking suits hanging for sale in long rows along the sidewalk—to the main bazaar.

That year the bazaar was still covered by the old vaulted stone ceiling which kept it delightfully cool. Round and cross-shaped openings allowed the sun to shine through and cast strange patterns of light and shadows into the crowded lanes. (In the never-ending efforts at modernization, the stone ceiling was replaced a year later by a glass roof which made the bazaar unbearably hot and deprived it of all its charm.)

Whenever we entered the bazaar, I would follow Najmeh past what seemed to be miles of shoe stalls, kitchen utensils, silver items and textiles. We always ended up in her favorite place: the rug bazaar—a whole village of rug-covered lanes stretching out endlessly in all directions. By that time, exhausted, we would end up sitting on a pile of rugs, drinking tea and eating delicious, tiny cucumbers with the merchants whom Najmeh charmed into showing us their choice collections.

Still, despite the impact Najmeh had on those who knew her, she had no close friends except for Maryna, an Armenian dressmaker. Often after our lessons, Najmeh wanted us to walk over to the decaying tenement where Maryna worked and lived with her two small children ever since her husband had left her years ago. Her one-room apartment, though crowded with shabby furniture and lined with her customers' clothes suspended on wire hangers from nails all along the walls, was neat and well organized. Whenever we came, she seemed delighted and quickly moved her ancient sewing machine and materials from her table to the bed so she could serve us coffee. Najmeh always wanted her grounds read by Maryna, since Najmeh could not predict her own future.

"I don't understand," I once said to Najmeh when she again eagerly handed her empty cup to Maryna. "How can you, with your intelligence and progressive ideas, be so superstitious?"

"But that has nothing to do with superstition," she said rather impatiently. "You can find truths in prophecies just as there are truths in dreams and fantasies."

"Why are you always so concerned with the future instead of living in the present and accepting what comes?" Maryna asked. "Don't you believe in destiny?"

"Of course I believe in destiny," Najmeh answered. "I feel as though I was always driven to do whatever I did, and am still doing, by some force, not by my free will. I am always trying to understand that force. Sometimes I think I am on the way to an understanding—there seem to be hints and signs every-where—in literature, in art, in dreams, yes, even in coffee grounds—which point to what I am looking for; and then again it evades me as though I had lost my way. I am afraid that time is slipping by without my ever getting anywhere...."

"But Najmeh, you found your faith. You are a Catholic...."

"But that's just it," Najmeh interrupted Maryna. "Doubts keep coming up and sometimes I feel as though the faith I have rejected is keeping me from getting complete satisfaction from my adopted one. Maybe we who have lost the faith in which we grew up are forever haunted by doubts...I thought I was doing what I had to do, but what if I misread the signs, I mean, imagine if I were wrong...."

Maryna glanced at me as though urging me to say or do something to relieve the burden of guilt which weighed on Najmeh, but I could think of nothing to say. After what seemed like a long silence, Najmeh shook her head as though forcefully dismissing her somber thoughts, smiled and brought up an entirely different subject.

A few days later, when I came for my lesson, the smile with which Najmeh always greeted me seemed artificial.

"What's wrong?" I asked.

"Oh, yesterday Reza and I had a dreadful fight. You cannot imagine. Now he did not want Leila to go to the kindergarten of the French Catholic School where she was registered, and as we argued Reza suddenly told me all the bad thoughts and resentments he has against me because of my attitude. Then he left home and he still has not come back."

Now Najmeh's doubts and guilt feelings surfaced again. She wondered whether she had any strength left to fight her environment. And did she have a right to fight it? Wasn't it her kismet? Could she dare to rebel against her fate? She told me that she had been to her church that morning, praying for guidance and strength, but there was no response. It was as though the saints over the altar were watching her coolly and saying: "You don't belong here. Look for solace among your own prophets."

She had to find out. She would return to the holy city of Meshed where she had gone with her father almost 18 years ago. She urged me to go with her. I agreed although I knew that I would not be able to visit the famous mosque or even the bazaar area which surrounds it, because it is positively danger-ous for a non-believer—man or woman—to be seen in the part of town adjoining the Holy Shrine.

The DC-3 flew for three hours over barren desert, but as we approached Meshed at sundown the golden dome of the Shrine of Iman and the many-colored tiling of the Gauhar Mosque emerged sparkling out of the drab city. The next morning Najmeh donned a black *chador* over her fashionable white suit, practiced for a while in front of a mirror the traditional way of clutching it under the eyes, and then left for the Shrine.

She returned sooner than I expected, bursting into the room and throwing herself on the bed. I stood staring at her. Her face was smudged, her suit dirty, her stockings torn. And then she told me what had happened.

"It was so beautiful in the Mosque. When I knelt before the Kabah (the Islamic altar facing Mecca), and as 'Allah AlAkhbar' (Allah is the greatest) resounded all around me, slowly the words and movements of prayer came back to me and I started to recite the *surahs* I had memorized in my childhood. It all came back to me so easily, and although tears were running down my cheeks, a sensation of tremendous strength and well-being filled me. As I repeated my prayers more and more fervently, I had a sensation of floating in a wonderful harmony, and Allah was all around me.

"Then, faintly, as if from far away I heard rumbling and voices, but nothing could enter the blissful circle which had enclosed me—until I felt myself grabbed, lifted into the air, carried out of the mosque and harshly dropped on the cobblestones of the courtyard. More and more people gathered around me, angry faces shouting, 'haram, haram,' (shame, shame). Someone threw my *chador* in my face and two men started to beat and kick me; it was so awful I wanted to die. And then, over the roar of the mob and the pounding of my heart, I heard a man's voice, loud and scolding. All became quiet; the men stepped aside and I saw an old bearded *mullah* bending over me. He helped me up, handed me my *chador* and told me to leave quickly. I hurriedly wrapped the *chador* around me and tried to run—it was so painful at first—but I ran as fast as I could, out of the courtyard and along the street until a taxi came along. And only then I realized what had happened. When I was praying so ardently, lowering and lifting my chest in the rhythm of the prayer, that *chador* was in my way. I am not used to it anymore and, without thinking, I laid it aside so that I could more easily give in to the movements of the prayers. And all these pious men, in the midst of their worship, were shocked to see a woman's head shamelessly uncovered in the holiest of the Houses of God."

Najmeh was exhausted but not wounded. When she came out of the bathroom, after cleaning her bruises and showering, she seemed her old self again. Laughing, she said, "At least I have it now, the final proof that I am a Moslem no longer. I am no longer capable of wearing a *chador* when I pray to Allah."

When we returned to Tehran, Najmeh found Reza at home; soon everything seemed to be going well again. As usual, Najmeh had won her argument and Reza had given in: Leila would be going to Jeanne d'Arc school.

At that time my life in Tehran became very busy so that I had to reduce my Persian lessons to once a week. Najmeh and I still did errands together or visited Maryna, but there were fewer occasions for our long talks. I did notice, however, that Najmeh was getting increasingly tense and restless. Every time I came to her house there was a change. She was trading her living room rug for a new one; she bought a new chair; she kept moving the furniture around, never satisfied that the house looked as she wanted it to. But in those days I was so

121

preoccupied with other concerns that I did not pay much attention to it.

Later, whenever I thought of Najmeh I tried to remember at what point I became apprehensive, as though suddenly seized by an intangible premonition of tragedy. It must have been in the late summer of 1960 that Najmeh was in perpetual motion, feverishly driven to undertake new tasks she kept imposing on herself. She took on more and more students among the garbage collectors. She worked on a Persian reader for illiterate adults. And she became overanxious about Leila, insisting on taking her to and from school instead of letting her ride the school bus with the other children.

One day when I came to her house I noticed that she had dark rings under her eyes, and I asked her what was wrong.

"I hardly slept last night," she said. "I tried to clean out my desk. All my things are in such disorder."

"You work too hard—you are completely exhausted," I said. "Why do you have to do everything at once?"

"Because there are so many things I must do," she answered, "and there is so little time to do them."

I laughed. "What's the hurry? You are only twenty-nine years old."

"Almost thirty," she answered with that forced smile that now often made me uneasy.

A week later, when we had planned to go to the bazaar after my lesson, she said, "Not today, Maria, I am too busy," and she showed me some material laid out on her dining room table.

"That's for Leila. I am making her four new dresses for school."

"Why does she need four dresses now?" I asked. "She has so many clothes."

"I have already cut the material so I must finish them today. Tomorrow morning early I want to dry-clean my draperies and the upholstery of my living room furniture. Look, they have already delivered the benzine I ordered; it's the finest on the market." She pointed to a metal drum standing in the courtyard. "I have so much work to do—and so little time...."

She must have noticed that I was disappointed and uneasy. "Never mind, Maria. I should be finished by ten or eleven, so why don't you come back around this time tomorrow? This was not a good lesson anyway, I was absentminded...."

That night, worrying about Najmeh kept me awake. Since she had stopped talking to me about her feelings of guilt and despondency, there was no way I could help her. I decided not to return to her for a few days; maybe she needed some time alone to do all the things she so obsessively felt she now had to do. But the next morning my apprehension was so gnawing that I had to see her.

Driving down Naderi Street, I was stopped by the police. The block around Najmeh's house was closed off and there was a dense crowd on the sidewalk. All I could see were fire engines and police cars and, above, a dark cloud of smoke. "A fire at the Ashgars," a bystander told me, but no one seemed to know any details. I made my way to Maryna's.

"It was the benzine," she said sobbing. "I had just left my house when I heard the explosion. I must have known what had happened because I started running, running toward Najmeh's house. When I got there flames were shooting out of her living room windows. The police and fire engines came immediately. The flames had not reached Leila's room, so they were able to save her. Reza was not there—apparently he had not come home last night." And, shuddering, she added in a barely audible voice, "I saw Najmeh. I stood right there as they carried her out—there was hardly anything left of her. She looked so tiny under the blanket."

The next day a Mass was said for Najmeh at her church. Very few people were there. Reza, leaning against a wall, was weeping loudly. When I walked over to him and took his hand, he stared at me distractedly and whispered, "My family would not come, not even to say good-bye to Najmeh. Mother said that Allah has punished her for having become an infidel."

I never went near Najmeh's house again. Maryna told me that everything that had belonged to her had burned—her desk, her papers, her living room furniture, her clothes, her rugs. The furniture in the other rooms as well as Reza's and Leila's clothes were untouched by the fire.

"Everything Najmeh worked for is destroyed," Maryna said. "Now Reza's mother will raise Leila as a good Moslem girl."

I asked for a picture of Najmeh. There was none.

Growing Time

Teresa Brun Ancel

The seeds lie waiting in the warm, dark earth. They send out tentative roots and shoots, seeking moisture, sun, life. They uncurl tenderly from their cores like the fists of slow-awakening babies and reach up, up into light.

Her cousin Betsy is fighting a war with cancer. Her niece is thinking of having an affair. There are already ten of them in the house with more to come. It is two days before Christmas and outside there's an ice storm raging.

Joanna stands at the kitchen sink washing yet another mound of dirty dishes and looking out of the window. The path from the house to the road must be a solid sheet of ice by now, impossible to navigate, and somebody will have to go out there and chop it up lest the mailman or the late arrivals break a leg. Doug, never driven by worry or guilt, is taking a nap. Joanna, hands immersed in hot soapy water, listens to the children argue in another room as they decorate the tree. She watches the unremitting, icy rain, and dreams of roses.

Roses signify love. Prom corsages of tiny pink ones wrapped in baby's breath. A red anniversary bouquet. In the spring she will make Doug build a trellis over the front steps and plant red roses to climb it. She will have more of them trailing over the front fence. And she will plant a yellow rose bush in the backyard. Every day, all summer, she will have cut flowers in the house, in every room and among them will be roses.

Betsy is losing her hair from the chemo. It comes out in clumps. They find it on the rug, on the pillows of the couch. When the dog, Mingo, sheds they complain. They say they're sorry they ever got him. They argue about whose turn it is to vacuum. Silently they gather Betsy's hair and bury it in the kitchen garbage can.

Betsy's husband, Lenny, jokes about grinding up apricot pits in the blender—instant Laetrile cocktail. He has a whole comedy routine about the oncologist, a morose and lanky man who never smiles. He has them rolling in the aisles when he talks about the other patients in the surgeon's office. There is a woman he calls The Stage Mother who tries to push her daughter through without waiting her turn. There is The Town ·Crier who reads the tabloids out loud, paying particular attention to the bloodiest crimes and methods of death, and somehow drawing a perverted strength and hope from that.

Joanna rinses and stacks the dishes and resolves that this time, when the summer finally comes, she will weed. She will not let the coarse grass and the dandelions grow between her flowers to soak up the needed nutrients and choke the life out of the things she so carefully plants. She will be diligent on a daily basis. She will stake her peonies so the frailer stems don't break and they don't fall over onto the muddy ground to rot or be eaten by worms. She will spray and water. She won't let her own procrastinating nature and the lassitude of summer overtake her. This time she will be vigilant so all her flowers, and not just the hardiest, will survive.

Joanna dries her hands and draws the kitchen curtain. She doesn't like the dark of storms, the early winter night. It makes her feel the house is under siege. It's childish to think she can shut out unpleasant things. In the winter she plans her garden. She looks through catalogues, draws diagrams, makes lists. She is resigned to her own nature.

Doug sometimes acts furious with her. "Nobody can be happy all the time!" he yells. "You have to just leave people alone. Life is not perfect. You're not responsible for everything." She knows he's not really angry. He worries about her feelings when things don't work out. He says she has to learn to toughen up.

Joanna is a great planner. She looks ahead. Months ago she planned this holiday. She wrote out menus. She made gift lists and guest lists and lists of things to clean. Cakes and pies and cookies are baking in the oven. The house is redolent with the smell of vanilla and cinnamon. The biggest turkey in America is defrosting and taking up half the refrigerator. She has bought additional decorations for the tree so that it will be more glittery than ever. As far back as last summer she started shopping for the presents. Now they are carefully wrapped and waiting under the tree. Everyone is getting something that, during the year, sometimes in the most casual way and never with expectation, they had mentioned they wanted. Yes, she wants people to be happy all the time.

Mike and Olivia are upstairs fighting. Joanna can't hear them. But she can feel it. The tension that came into the house with them, that follows them from room to room, is now drifting down the stairs from the bedroom where they have shut themselves off from holiday preparations. It's not the kind of fight she understands, hot and quickly over. This is a blight, a smothering animosity built on old resentments and a new, more hurtful uncaring.

Olivia said earlier, in a fierce whisper when they were alone together for a moment, "If it wasn't for AIDS I would have had an affair by now."

The children came running in and Joanna never had a chance to question and to sympathize, to explore solutions with Olivia. She is left feeling frustrated and sad.

She hopes the Rose of Sharon won't be invaded by Japanese beetles again. Just as the buds burst into bloom they fell to the ground, bitten off too soon. All summer the trees stood vulnerable and denuded as the beautiful pink and white flowers dropped down. There was nothing she could do to save them.

As she puts the last dish on the draining board she hears a crash in the living room. Katherine begins to cry. Doug is startled from his nap on the couch and begins to yell. Lenny comes in for the broom and dust pan. He is laughing, pantomiming chaos, and they smile at each other, conspirators in a world gone mad. Doug comes stomping in, hair rumpled, feeling put upon and righteous. He gets his boots from the utility room and stomps out again. Now that he hasn't been allowed his uninterrupted sleep he might as well go chop the ice from the driveway and the paths.

With the ringing of the bell they all converge in the hallway by the front door. Every one of them is eager to be on hand to greet the arrivals. Only Olivia's one-year old baby is not there, napping now so he can be passed from adult to adult and played with and adored later. The children cluster together,

Joanna's daughter, Katherine, at eleven is almost as tall as her brother and awkward with it, all arms and legs and eyes. Steve, Betsy's fifteen year old son, and Margaret, Olivia's five year old daughter, who has a crush on him and trails him like a shadow are flushed with excitement. The adults, including Joanna, are as excited as the children because once everyone is there the holiday officially begins.

And there they finally are. First her sister, Andrea, and the latest boyfriend, Sam, come in on a gust of icy wind. Joanna has never seen Sam before and has been curious to meet him. Andrea has always dated, and twice married, starving artists, hopeful actors, down-at-luck musicians. Andrea has described Sam as a solid and sensible lawyer type in a deprecating tone. He is a tall, middle-aged man with thin, sandy hair. He is wearing a dark suit, a paisley tie, a navy cashmere coat. Everyone else is dressed in plaid shirts and sweaters, jeans and cords. He doesn't seem ill at ease. He hands Doug a bag filled with white wine and a bottle of Drambuie. He has a poinsettia for Joanna. She feels she will like him, and Andrea won't for long.

As soon as their coats are off and they begin to move toward the living room the doorbell rings again. Like actors in a play waiting for their cues they freeze in place. They turn back toward the door in a tangled, laughing mass as Andrea's son Mark and his wife Janice come in shaking off ice pellets, hair glistening and damp. Their arms are filled with packages to be put under the tree. Again they go through the ritual of hugs and kisses, bumping each other awkwardly because there seem to be so many of them in the small space of the hall. "This is quite a reception," Mark says beaming. "Bring on the fatted calf."

This time they make it to the living room and are placing packages under the tree, shaking boxes with their names on them and making wild guesses on the contents when the doorbell rings again. The children stampede out of the room, the adults following. Doug curses good-naturedly as Mingo tangles himself around everybody's feet barking noisily. "Get down, you idiot. Get out of the way—get out!" he bellows as Steve pulls open the door and Pop, Doug's father, walks in. Megan, Andrea's daughter and Laurence, Joanna's son press in behind him.

"You should show your daddy more respect, Uncle Doug,"

Andrea teases as she gives him a kiss. "I know you're not talking to me because I'm your favorite niece. It must be your horrible son you're yelling at." She turns and punches Laurence on the arm and he gives a tug to a strand of her fly-away red hair.

"Aren't you two ever going to outgrow that?" Joanna scolds, secretly glad they haven't. Both kids are on winter break from college, both freshmen, and full of themselves because they count themselves among the adults now.

"They've been squabbling all the way here," Pop grumbles, obviously pleased rather than upset. 'Drive faster, drive slower, I'm hungry, you just ate, put the window up, put the window down—I thought *old* people were supposed to be crotchety... if it wasn't so darn cold out, I think I would have gotten out and walked."

"Why Pop, you know you enjoyed every minute of it," says Megan taking him by the arm and steering him toward the couch. "You sit down and I'll get you a nice hot drink while you tell everyone what wonderful company we were."

"And what a great driver I am," says Laurence.

"Well, if I'm going to tell tall tales I might as well make them real whoppers."

Laurence and Megan took trains from their schools and met in the city at Pop's apartment. Pop is too old to drive alone now and Laurence has driven everyone up in Pop's car. He has driven a sizable distance for the first time, over a hundred miles with a two-week old license in his pocket. Laurence doesn't know it, but Pop is giving him the car as a Christmas present. The car is older than Laurence. Joanna knows what Pop will do and she's happy for Laurence, but afraid. Accidents happen.

Joanna always overplants her garden. She goes for quantity, not artistic effect. She overplants from fear that nothing will grow. Every mass of blooms is a surprise that fills her with gladness, every seed ungerminated is a betrayal. She feels almost as if she has a pact with nature. She will be unstinting as she sows, lavish with her care on every plant, and then they must thrive and overrun the beds in riotous abundance. She breathes in the colors of her flowers as well as their scents. She seeds with wild abandon, forgetting or ignoring her winter charts and lists. Marigolds grow among the zinnias. Cosmos spring up among the bleeding hearts. Tomatoes thrive amid pansies and day-lilies. Purples and oranges bloom side by side, tall stems and short entangled. She doesn't mark what she has planted. Every year she is surprised by which and where flowers grow. Every year she claims her garden is the best it's ever been.

There are seventeen people in the house. They will all stay till the day after Christmas. The younger ones will line up sleeping bags in the attic. The living room couch will be pulled out. Cots will be set up. There is so much to do. And she will have to find a moment to take Laurence aside and speak to him about driving safely. She will have to speak to Andrea about where to put Sam. In the same room, in the same bed? This is a problem she hasn't foreseen. She will have to warn Andrea about Olivia and Mike. Or should she say anything—maybe it will all blow over? Maybe she will tell Olivia to tell her mother what's going on.

Sam borrows a shirt and jeans from Doug. The men are going out. They will look at the stars, see the cabinet Doug is building in the garage, bring in logs for the fireplace. They will escape the house chores, and the women, like truant school boys.

The women are in the kitchen pulling out silverware and dishes to set the table. They are making salad, tasting things in pots. The women smile at each other as the men go out. They envision the activities of the men to be a bonding ritual, a hurdle they must pass before they can talk to each other. The women know these men don't talk as easily as they do. The men smile at each other as they pass the women all talking at the same time, all flushed and busy in the warmth of the kitchen. They see this as a bonding ritual, too. It is as mysterious as tribal rites, as comforting and joyous as the patterns of an intricate and familiar dance they all mastered long ago.

Joanna counts the faces at her table, including the ones who aren't there. Two years ago her mother died. Ten years ago Doug lost his mother. When Joanna was eight her parents divorced and now her father is a once-a-year postcard from California. She wants more faces at the table, not fewer. Next year she will tell the children to bring friends from college. Maybe Mark and Janice will have a baby by then. Even this year she can do more. Maybe she will invite the elderly couple who live down the road for Christmas dinner. She'll invite Mrs. Hanson and her infrequently visiting daughter. She'll invite the Rileys whose parents bought a condo in Florida and are gone for the entire winter. She can easily feed twenty-three people. She can easily feed thirty. Joanna always cooks too much.

This summer she will plant a second rhododendron on the other side of the path. Six months before her mother died, she found one in the refuse room of her building. She brought it over and insisted Joanna plant it. It looked so wilted and brown Joanna had been sure it wouldn't survive. But it had filled out, grown huge and bushy and sprouted crimson flowers. The children still call it Nana Irene's rhododendron. Sometimes she feels her mother knows how beautifully it bloomed and she is filled with a comforting joy. It's silly, but sometimes she talks to the plant, says things she would say to her mother if her mother were still alive. That rhododendron has heard about the children's grades, the lost baby, Joanna's struggles with a diet. She will plant another for Doug's mother, the grandmother the children hardly remember.

This year she will plant more gladiolus and more tulip bulbs. Last year something ate most of the tulips. Luckily the hyacinths and daffodils had spread and had filled the empty spots. Betsy had helped her set out the daffodils when they'd first bought the house. Andrea's first husband had helped build the grape arbor over the picnic table. Both children had a tree to celebrate their birth, Laurence a red maple and Katherine a magnolia. She will plant nothing for Betsy because Betsy will be there in the spring to plant it for herself.

They are sprawled on the chairs and floor and couch in front of the fireplace. They have eaten too much but they are eating popcorn anyway. They are arguing companionably over the answers to Trivial Pursuit. Joanna loves board games a lot of people can play together. She loves the comfortable squabbling they all indulge in when they get together.

Joanna is lost in plans for her garden. In the middle of the game she says,"This summer let's plant several varieties of tomatoes. That way we can figure out which ones will do best." The adults laugh and the children groan. They are used to the way Joanna's mind works. She has unexpectedly propelled them into spring. As the ice storm rages outside they are looking forward to all that digging and fencing and weeding and complaining they will do. They remember last year. Joanna always plants so much that they give tomatoes away to anyone who will take them. They eat tomatoes for breakfast lunch and dinner. The children start to sing "Attack of the Killer Tomatoes." Sam joins them. It is not a Christmas carol but warms her heart in the same way. She is not listening to the words. She is hearing their voices rise and blend in song.

Mike says, "Olivia and I planned to start a garden this summer. We've never tried it before and we'll probably make a mess, but—"

"I'll help," Joanna offers quickly. Olivia looks unsure and glum.

"Let's plant some pumpkins out in back next year, on the edge of the field where the wild flowers bloom," Betsy says suddenly.

Joanna feels a surge of joy. Every time Betsy seems to forget about the cancer, Joanna feels as if she is scoring one for their side. Every time Betsy looks down the tunnel of the present into the possibility of a future, Joanna feels the elation of hope. Wishful thinking? Joanna doesn't care. Thinking good thoughts must lead to good results, or so she persists in wanting to believe.

Lenny jokes about setting out some marijuana plants for Betsy, but luckily Pop is sleeping and doesn't hear him. Andrea gestures him to be silent in front of the children.

Laurence says, which makes Joanna flush with pleasure, that in spite of the pain in the neck they are, he can't think of his childhood without thinking of his mother's gardens. Someday, Joanna hopes and is almost sure, he will plant his own.

"You always looked like a kid whose mother was thinking about pruning trees as she cut your hair," says Andrea.

They are growing heavy with food and drink and relaxation. It has been a perfect evening.

Joanna knows the good feeling won't last. At some point, while they are all together, Megan will fight with Olivia or Andrea. Laurence will take Pop's car, now his, and drive out on the icy night roads and Joanna will worry. The children will get teary and argumentative from too much excitement and candy. Maybe Olivia will announce she's leaving Mike. Maybe they will finally fight with words and embarrass themselves and everybody else and it will all blow over. Maybe Betsy will feel worse before, please God, she's better. The house will go from feeling cheery and warm and complete to being messy and too crowded. Doug, who thrives on order and solitude, will get irritable from too long a time with too many people. As Joanna's catalogues spill off tables and onto floors, as Christmas wrap piles up in corners, and as the children's scattered toys are never put away, he will glumly kick things out from underfoot or retreat to the garage to brood in silence.

Joanna sees beyond that. That it is always growing time is the truest thing Joanna knows. It is the thing that gets her past the hurts, both great and small. The planting of a garden is an act of hope and life against the knowledge of calamity and death. So Joanna plans her garden. Especially in the coldest season.

Notes on The Byrdcliffe Writers

JOSEPH KEEFE has written a book-length study of James Gould Cozzens and has been awarded fellowships by both the State University of New York and the National Endowment for Humanities. For the past twenty-five years he has taught literature and writing at the Ulster County Community College in Stone Ridge. He lives in Woodstock with his wife, Jane, the owner-director of the Country Mouse School.

TERESA BRUN ANCEL, born in Warsaw, Poland, is a free-lance writer who has published numerous short stories and non-fiction articles and has worked as an editor and advertising copywriter. She lives in New York and Woodstock and accomplishes her work with the invaluable help (both literary and domestic) of her husband, Richard, and her son, Jordan.

MARIA BAUER, born in Prague, Czechoslovakia, first came to Woodstock in 1941 as a Byrdcliffe tenant of Mrs. Whitehead. Later, after her husband joined the foreign service, she lived in Iran, France, Egypt, and India. Her first book, *Beyond the Chestnut Trees*, an alternate selection of the Literary Guild, was published in 1984, the paperback edition in 1986. She and her husband live and work in Woodstock and Washington, D.C.

SUSAN SUTLIFF BROWN divides her time between Woodstock where she summers and Florida where she teaches English, Creative Writing, and American Literature at a Community College. Ms. Brown, who holds a Ph.D in English Literature, was the recipient of a McKnight sabbatical grant and grants from the National Endowment for the Humanities for her scholarly work on James Joyce. She is currently completing a book on Joyce's use of geometry and physics in *Ulysses*, but she prefers writing fiction.

JO McKIM CHALMERS grew up on the Canal Zone, Panama. She started "scribbling" when she had the measles. She now wishes she had spent half of the time writing that she has spent in the Theatre. And looks forward each summer, with considerable joy, to the ten lively and rewarding weekly meetings with the Byrdcliffe Writers, up on Guardian Mountain.

LESLIE GERBER was born in Brooklyn in 1943. He has lived in the Hudson Valley for twenty years. He was graduated from Brooklyn College with a degree in creative writing. Most of his writing since then has been music criticism, largely for *Fanfare* magazine and the *Woodstock Times*. He is also a classical music broadcaster for WDST in Woodstock, and runs Parnassus Records, dealing in rare classical recordings.

ADELE LeBLANC was born and raised in Alabama. She moved to New York to marry a Yankee. She has followed an unfocused career pattern which has included teaching and singing in nightclubs in the South, a stint as head librarian at Harcourt Brace and as vice president in a large Executive Search firm in New York City. She is finally earning her living as a writer.

MARY LEONARD lives with Jerry, Josh, and Nicole in a two-story frame house in uptown Kingston. In the summers she finds peace and inspiration on the old Byrdcliffe colony's mountainside above Woodstock.

TARA McCARTHY writes language arts, literature, and social studies textbooks and serves as an educational consultant and writer-in-residence in elementary schools. She is also the author of eleven trade books—both fiction and non-fiction—for young readers. She is still "working on" the novels and plays she began 25 years ago, when she settled in Woodstock.

SCOTT MORGAN studied in the Graduate Writing Program at S.U.N.Y. Albany. He is presently completing a novel, *Island of Sacrifice*.

GENE PATTERSON, producing and editing TV/radio programs for a long time, helped put words in the mouths of Ma Perkins, detective Mark Saber, Valiant Lady, and Jonathan Winters. Alongside Betty Crocker, he served with distinction under General Mills. He has been hopelessly involved with the Byrdcliffe Writers since their founding.

R. L. TUCKER, retired educator, beginning poet, erstwhile prose writer, is pleased to be working with an intelligent but down-to-earth group.